NATURALISTIC PLANTING DESIGN

The Essential Guide

NATURALISTIC PLANTING DESIGN

The Essential Guide

Nigel Dunnett

filbert press

07 Foreword by Piet Oudolf

08 Introduction: Planting for People

22 From the Beginning

52 Understanding Contemporary Naturalism

70 Reading Nature

104 Planting Design Toolkit

164 Future Nature

208 Cultivation Guidelines

230 Epilogue

Further Reading 232 / Acknowledgements 233 / Index 234 / About the Author 239

FOREWORD

I've known Nigel since he started out as a young researcher and have followed his progress ever since. We've attended numerous workshops, seminars and conferences together and, as I get to know Nigel better, I realise just how similar our views and outlooks on planting design are, especially when it comes to naturalistic plantings provoking strong and wonderful emotions in people. I have been impressed by the way he makes beautiful gardens and landscapes that have the feel of nature but are underpinned by detailed scientific research.

Nigel is one of the few designers who works in private gardens and is also driven to bring natural planting into our cities and public places. It's not an easy thing to do, as I know well, but in our changing climate it matters and it's where Nigel's 'low-input, high-impact' ideas are so important. There are many exceptional examples of his public work including roof gardens, rain gardens and urban meadows in the pages that follow.

I was interested to read about Nigel's early interest in plants. He describes how he was captured by the wonder and awe of experiencing natural landscapes from a young age. These formative experiences led to decades of observation and research into wild plant communities. In one of the most fascinating parts of the book, Nigel looks at a single meadow in China and brings out from it an incredible number of principles that he then bases his planting methods upon.

The world of naturalistic planting design is one that I have been involved with all of my working life. It's a world of endless possibilities and a source of limitless joy. It's a field that's constantly evolving, and we must always seek to renew, expand the boundaries of what is possible, and build exciting new concepts on the foundations of what's come before. Without doubt the book provides a springboard for naturalistic design to evolve still further and will encourage a whole new generation of designers and gardeners to embrace new and fresh thinking as they work with environmentally aware approaches to planting.

Piet Oudolf
Hummelo, December 2018

INTRODUCTION

We are bound to nature, tied tight. It's at our very core, in our blood, inescapable. It's integral to us: it's what makes us feel complete. We need it, but that's not surprising: of course we do – we are part of it! The human desire to make gardens, and to create green environments in even the bleakest of surroundings, is the supreme expression of that innate connection to the wild. To design with plants, to make our own expressions of the natural world, somehow brings us closer to that inbuilt yearning to be part of the bigger scheme of life. For me, this is why designing with plants is very important – indeed, I could go further and say that it is essential to our very future. My aim is not just to create something functional, or to fill a space, or to copy nature, and it's even not just to make something beautiful. It's to create something that tugs deep inside us, at an element that's fundamental. Above all, it's to provoke emotions: hugely positive ones. And it's an amazing thing when a landscape, garden or planting I've created makes that happen.

PLANTING FOR PEOPLE

This book is all about creating plant-rich gardens and landscapes, and working in tune with nature to create the most beautiful, wonderful, joyful, uplifting and engaging places; making spaces that resonate with natural forms, not just filling them with green. It's about celebrating the energy and power of the natural world, and the relationship we have with it. And it's about being liberated and empowered ourselves, through working in an exuberant way with plants. It's my belief that carefully considered naturalistic planting touches those parts of us that other types of planting just can't reach. We interact with it in a different way, and it potentially provokes different types of feelings within us. So this book presents a guide to designing with plants, combining beauty and meaning with a fresh environmental outlook, to create places that are in tune with nature and their surroundings.

Above and opposite below: The High Line in New York has demonstrated the economic, social and environmental benefits of dramatic green interventions in even the most densely built up environments. Design: James Corner Field Operations & Piet Oudolf.

Previous page: Using this as inspiration combined with an understanding of how plant communities work, we have unrivalled opportunities to make our own beautiful and breath-taking examples of designed plant communities. Urban Meadows, Queen Elizabeth Olympic Park, London. Design: Nigel Dunnett

One of my primary aims in designing with plants is to produce an emotional response in the viewer. What I strive for is an overwhelming sense of beauty, of warmth, of awe, of drama, and of fascination. But I believe it can go a lot further than that, and be truly life-enhancing and even life-changing, because it can drill through the layers of inhibition and convention that we all build up and release pure, child-like unsullied joy and freedom in the same way that painting, sculpture and music do. But unlike any other medium, plants are living and dynamic, and the composition changes over time. That's both a very exciting idea, but at the same time challenging too.

Planting design as an art form

When I work with plants I have a couple of maxims. The first is 'Planting design as an art form: tuned to nature'. The 'tuned to nature' part of it refers to working in what's loosely termed a naturalistic way with plants. However, in the world of naturalistic, ecologically inspired planting design, it's easy to get bogged down in all the technicalities. Year by year, these seem to be getting more and more complex, with myriad confusing terms and methods. Indeed, sometimes it seems to be all about the minute detail of *how* to do it, rather than the overwhelming arguments for *why* to do it. It's crucial not to lose sight of the why, and when it comes to thinking about that the first part of the maxim becomes relevant. Let's not forget that planting has to move, arrest and delight people in the way that a work of art does. And let's put that right at the top of the list of priorities, because in our increasingly crowded world, where we have to fit more and more into ever smaller spaces, gardens have to work first and foremost for people if they are to achieve anything.

It's crucial that we find ways to integrate the naturalistic approach into those smaller spaces as well as the large-scale applications. We need to think about intimate space, and to design and work at the human scale – and I believe that's true regardless of how big the area is that we have at our disposal. This is why, despite the strong environmental ethic running through this book, it's about people first, and is uncompromising in expounding a strong naturalistic planting philosophy. This is nothing new, of course. But we have been in the orbit of what has come to be called contemporary naturalistic planting design (or more specifically new perennial planting) for several decades now. This term actually covers a very wide range of styles and approaches, each with its own jargon and technical design principles. An important aim of this book is to cut through some of this complexity and to distil things down to what I hope is a more straightforward set of terms and principles. However, more than that, it's time to review where we are with the whole naturalistic planting movement. It's time to move things on, and to use the principles of the new perennial movement to embrace the whole plant world and not just perennials.

Top: It's possible to create uplifting, immersive, naturalistic environments in even the most urban of settings as here at the Barbican, London. Planting design: Nigel Dunnett

Planting design as an essential

My second maxim is at first glance quite different – 'Planting design as an essential: creating healthy cities and livable places'. This might seem a contradiction to the first one, but the two are completely interlinked. We need to move away from the notion that planting design is a decorative thing that softens our built environment and while it's a nice thing to have, it's also a bit frivolous. Through my work I've sought to promote a very different viewpoint: rather than being an add-on at the end, the creation of a plant-rich human landscape is actually the essential starting point; rather than being something that is perhaps a bit lightweight, it is in fact deadly serious. It's a crucial element for creating healthy and livable places, whether in the heart of the city or in the remote countryside, in public spaces or private gardens. We need to move from a 'nice-to-have' to a non-negotiable 'must-have'.

Planting design is essential because of the many benefits that the combination of soils and plants brings to us and to the wider web of life. And it's a huge new opportunity for planting that's tuned to nature, because although any sort of planting will, I suppose, give some sort of benefit, when it's done according to the principles in this book it will function to the maximum and be sustainable in the widest sense. This potential hasn't even begun to be met to any significant extent, so the field is wide open – and it's a great chance for beautiful and creative

Above: Exuberant infiltration of plants and vegetation into as many aspects of everyday life as possible allows us to re-establish a connection with nature that has been all but lost for many people.

planting design to leap over the garden fence and the park boundary and to invade the streets and other places that just a relatively short while ago would have seemed unthinkable. Again we come back to our dual goal: we have the chance to make our everyday living environments so much more healthy and environmentally positive, and astounding at the same time.

Left: Bringing joyful and colourful naturalistic planting into everyday life can unlock our deep, often child-like, emotional connection with nature, whether we know it or not. Housing Estate, Sheffield with Nigel Dunnett's Pictorial Meadows seed mix.

Inspired by nature

If you work in a naturalistic way, then by definition you are inspired by nature – but this can mean many different things. For some it's literal and focuses on re-creating the essence of specific named landscapes or plant communities in some detail. This can follow a 'biogeographic' route, in which the plant communities of a region of the world are studied and adapted in a stylized way to be used in ecologically suitable conditions elsewhere. For example, in his 2017 book *Sowing Beauty*, James Hitchmough provides extensive species lists of different biogeographic North American, European, Asian and South African plant communities that could form the basis of new plantings, inspired by actual assemblages that occur in the wild.

As part of this biogeographic approach we might also include the native plant movements around the world which propose that designed plantings should only be composed of native plant species appropriate to the region or locality. In the purest form of restoration ecology or habitat creation, designers will work only with native species in representations of local plant communities. This whole approach may be inspired by aesthetic delight at particular landscapes or plant communities, but it is essentially a deeply scientific endeavour to then work out how to re-create these plant communities in a designed situation, often in areas thousands of miles from where they occur naturally. So, an element of the above 'natural inspiration' for planting design is what I would call 'taxonomic' – it's about making lists of plants that compose specific natural plant communities and then using them as the basis for the new designed plantings. The argument is that these species have evolved together, and naturally work together.

Of course there's also a completely different way of thinking about natural inspiration. Rather than a 'taxonomic ecology', I also like to think in terms of a 'visual ecology'. For me, it's not about trying to re-create something that I might have seen in the wild. Instead, it's about using the forms, textures, colours and aesthetics

Above: My main inspiration for planting design comes from meadow plant communities in the wild. Here is a beautiful colour combination of *Iris bulleyana* and *Persicaria bistorta* in a field in Sichuan, China.

that reflect the way plants arrange themselves in natural plant communities, but seeing this as only a starting point in building up an ecological aesthetic. I want to take advantage of the huge range of plants that are available to make new types of designed natures: a sort of *human nature*. Further than that, in this uncertain time of climate and environmental change I want to make a sort of *future nature* that's adapted to the kinds of conditions we might expect to be living with in years and decades ahead. So, this book is about evoking nature, capturing the spirit of a landscape, and looking at methods and techniques for integrating natural elements into what may be highly designed, artificial and contemporary spaces.

Learning from plant communities

Above all, it's about capturing and promoting the most profound and uplifting emotional responses that natural landscapes can stimulate in us. To do that, I believe that there is no really no need to re-create any specific real plant communities. It's a matter of understanding the visual cues or triggers that make us think that something has a natural quality about it.

So when I say that I am inspired by nature, more than anything it's about being inspired by the emotional response that I gain from certain types of natural experience. But the inspiration is also about something else: the dynamic, energetic, driving life-force of plant communities and how they work as a system. Because that's what they are – an interacting system of parts that come together to make the whole. Understanding the basic mechanisms by which natural plant communities work is the most straightforward way in which to achieve sustainable plantings that require minimal resources to keep them going – I call it 'high-impact, low-input' planting, and it's the basis for the way that I work.

Above: Large expanses of the same thing, although dramatic at first view, soon become monotonous and over-powering.

Filling space or making space?

Most advice about naturalistic and plant community-based design seems to be mainly about filling space – in other words, rolling out a particular plant mix or assemblage to occupy a given area. But as well as merely *filling* space, in the same way that floorboards or carpet occupy a floor, we also need to think about planting design as being about *making* space – in other words, about creating the actual room in the first place! Plant-rich gardens and landscapes need to structured and shaped with plants, as well as being packed full with them. So naturalistic planting design must be just as much about making naturalistic spaces as it is about the plantings that fill them.

Above: Striking combinations of colours, textures, forms and structures in a designed planting at the Barbican in London. Design: Nigel Dunnett

Opposite: The visual patterns in natural plant communities are the result of complex interactions between the plants themselves and the environmental 'forces' acting on the site. Understanding these is an important step in achieving sustainable plantings in the garden.

Perhaps because the prairie, steppe, meadow and other grassland plant communities and landscapes that have inspired much contemporary naturalistic planting design are themselves found in nature on a vast scale, many of the best-known examples of designed naturalistic planting are themselves extensive, filling whole fields in both private or public spaces. To visit these examples is certainly dramatic, but the experience can also be mentally draining. Ironically, the rich diversity that is apparent at the smaller scale can become monotonous when repeated over large areas. It's impressive, yes, but starts to lack spirit and spark. Large spaces filled with essentially the same thing provide for little in the way of ongoing engagement beyond the initial impression, spectacular though that may be. Repetition of the same elements over wide spaces means that what you see at first view is what you get at second, third and fourth view too.

Making intimate spaces

I am regularly asked whether this type of planting is suitable for small spaces too. The answer is yes! My approach is to be bold and dramatic, using plants to create uplifting, exciting and memorable designs that are sometimes subtle, sometimes vivid. There is one constant factor that I believe makes for the most effective planting design, regardless of the size of the space: intimacy. To fully engage with that deep human response to nature, it is necessary to work and think at the human scale: a scale that enables us to respond to and interact with our surroundings, and one in which we feel comfortable and secure. Even in the largest of areas, we need to create small-scale moments as the means by which we properly experience those spaces.

This is the point at which we need to introduce a fundamental piece of theoretical thinking that underpins everything in this book. It lies at the heart of my proposition that the artful naturalistic approach to planting design is the highest form of planting design, and why we always need to bear in mind the idea of intimate space and planting design at the human scale. This is the concept of evolutionary psychology, which attempts to explain how our current behaviours, preferences and everyday choices are in part determined with natural selection and our own evolution as a species.

Above: Creating intimate experiences at a human scale within naturalistic plantings, in even the largest of areas, is key to making them work for people. It's also the best way to approach their use in smaller spaces. These three examples from the author's garden show how small seating or gathering areas, and the use of exploratory paths can create that intimate feel. Simply placing a seat on the edge, half-in, half-out, encourages a more engaged and active experience.

I'm not a robot

Homo sapiens has been a distinct species for remarkably little time – only 25,000 years, according to some experts. That doesn't even register as the merest pin-prick of time in terms of life on earth. We evolved from other hominids that had perhaps been around for a few million years. Throughout this time, we and our ancestors lived intimately and indivisibly tied into the landscape and territorial range. It's only been in the last couple of thousand years that groups of people came together in communities of any size, and perhaps only in the last few hundred that significant numbers of people could be said to have lost their direct connection with the land. That's really only a handful of human generations, and absolutely nothing in terms of evolutionary time.

There's a substantial body of thought that proposes that large parts of our behaviour, preferences and actions are still governed by that evolutionary history; that our instincts as animals are buried beneath the thin veneer of consciousness and sensibility that we like to call free will, and it is the power of those instincts that ultimately hold sway. It's disturbing to think our decisions and choices that we consider to be the result of rational processes may actually be to some extent pre-determined. But, "You're not a robot or automaton," I hear you say, "you can override those basic drives through the force of your sophisticated intellect!" Probably true, but consider the actual strength of inbuilt instinct. The migration of birds across continents; the complexity of the bee-hive or ant-hill; the building of dams by beavers, and an infinite number of other examples. All unlearnt behaviours, mysteriously made possible by the diktat of the genetic code. It seems impossible that we should be the only species exempt from this.

Below: Savannah-like landscapes, with larger open spaces, views and sight-lines (prospect) that also have plenty of opportunities for shelter and cover (refuge) are naturally pleasing and comfortable to us because of our evolutionary past.

Introduction

One of the most powerful landscape and garden-related ideas to come out of evolutionary psychology is the concept of prospect-refuge, first proposed by Jay Appleton in his important 1975 book *The Experience of Landscape*. Appleton proposed that as a result of the vast amount of our evolutionary time being spent in intimate association with the landscape as hunter-gatherer societies, the most satisfactory and pleasing landscapes from the human viewpoint are those in which we can 'see without being seen'. In other words, landscapes that can be quickly seen, read and understood from a viewing point (prospect), but where this is done so from a point of safety (refuge). In evolutionary terms, we prefer easy-to-understand landscapes, where opportunities and threats can be easily seen from afar, and we like to experience them from places where we feel secure and safe from danger, especially from being attacked from behind. In other words, intimate space.

The idea of human-scale thinking is just one part of this. We need structure and order in our designed landscapes so that we can read them immediately. That's why simply filling large areas with random-looking naturalistic planting isn't really going to please us. Chaos doesn't work. Many of our preferences for what we like and don't like are at least in part in-built. Of course, this is controversial, and a lot of our preferences are also cultural and a result of who and where we are – it's the old argument of nature vs nurture. But there's a sufficient foundation there for me to be confident that much of what we will discuss in this book is universal – it's within all of us, waiting to be unlocked. It's primitive and often buried deep, but it's there. I believe that well-designed, naturalistic plantings have the power to unlock these primeval instincts. It's what I mean when I talk about the emotional response, and perhaps it's no coincidence that these are child-like feelings of liberation. Later in the book we shall look at how to translate the features of inspiring and legible natural landscapes into a planting design methodology that holds the key to this primitive unlocking.

Because this is about emotional response, in some ways it is a very personal thing, and the best way for me to explain it is to tell my own story. I hope that my own experiences speak to these wider universal truths.

Above: Smaller-scale landscapes such as this are full of 'prospect and refuge' and make us feel at ease, while having a great deal of visual interest.

Opposite: Naturalistic planting with intimate spaces at a human scale, can foster feelings of relaxation and well-ness even in the middle of a city, like these at the Barbican. Planting Design: Nigel Dunnett

FROM THE BEGINNING

I have been steeped in gardens and horticulture for as long as I can remember. It started out in a very simple way: I was overawed by the possibility of creating new life. I can remember it well, even though I must have been only four or five years old. My parents were both enthusiastic gardeners and they helped me take some pelargonium cuttings. The excitement of seeing new roots poking out of the base of the pots was a magical experience. A little later, I took a cutting from a weeping willow tree. This was eventually planted in our front garden and it grew up with me, increasing in height as I did, and giving me a great sense of personal involvement in bringing something into being. This led to a passion for growing things from seed – again all part of the excitement of bringing things to life.

EARLY ENCOUNTERS WITH PLANTS

At this stage my horticultural knowledge was very narrow, limited to what was easily available from seed. But I have to admit I was obsessive! In fact, as a teenager, my furtive bedtime reading consisted of endlessly poring over seed catalogues, fantasizing over all the different lettuce varieties, or types of marigold I could grow! My outlook was very traditional, and based on the garden books and TV programmes of the time. I loved seasonal bedding plants. I took huge pride in neatly cultivated, weed-free soil between my specimen plants, and nothing impressed me more than a freshly cut-back flower border at the end of the summer, all neat and tidy. I revelled in such a thing and, although I now work in a very different way, I never disregard the pleasure that 'traditional' gardening gives.

I never underrate the sheer pleasure that traditional horticulture gives to people.

In my teenage years my view was to change – and it happened completely by chance. My parents were members of the local gardening club and the annual outing was a trip to the Royal Horticultural Society's main garden at Wisley, in Surrey. After going round the gardens, the only way out was through the gift shop. I took a look through the huge gardening book selection and saw a small book that intrigued me, but not for obvious reasons. It was a little orange-spined Penguin paperback, with a picture of a house and exuberant garden on the front, and while it contained some photographs, it was mostly text. I bought it, probably out of some pretentious idea that if it was a Penguin book then it would carry with it some sort of intellectual aura! I read it on the bus trip home, and my eyes were suddenly opened to a whole new world. I had chanced upon *The Well-Tempered Garden* by Christopher Lloyd, and as the book unfolded, I began to realize that there was a whole gardening universe beyond the vegetable patch and the flower border of bedding plants. But most of all, for the first time, gardening was presented as something beyond 'jobs to do at the weekend' and an endless ritual of tasks and rigid practices. Instead, rules were made to be broken, received wisdom was there to be challenged, there was no right or wrong, and the possibilities for personal experimentation and trying things out were endless. Above all it was witty and irreverent, and I had never associated gardening with any words like that.

Here I do have to admit to a certain precociousness! From the age of 12 or 13 or so I set off on a personal voyage of discovery. I read and gardened as much as I could and visited as many gardens as possible. At school, I couldn't wait for the weekends when I would be away from the stifling constrictions of the classroom and outside in the fresh air with my hands in the soil, planting and cultivating. In those endless classroom confinements, my mind would be flying free and planning what I would be doing in the liberation of the garden. So really my gardening (and design) background was largely self-taught, gained through the experience of seeing it and doing it as well as reading about it.

Above: The contrast between very formal elements, and energetic wild planting is a Great Dixter trademark.

By the age of 18, when it came to deciding what to do at college, horticulture was my passion and I felt that I could learn all I needed to through my own personal exploration. I had already gained a depth of practical and theoretical knowledge, though I was still in a fairly narrow band of thinking – what might be considered as the cosy, tasteful, middle-class arts and crafts world of British gardening. So I didn't pursue any formal training in horticulture, garden design or landscape architecture (even though I knew that was where my future lay) but instead opted to achieve a scientific background in botany, plant science and ecology, because I thought I could never properly teach myself any of that in true depth. And I wanted this scientific background because of a second area of passionate interest that I had also had since I was very little: what might best be termed 'natural history'.

I grew up on the edge of the town of Ipswich, in the county of Suffolk, England. My parents had built their own bungalow on the busy main road into the town, on a plot of land that was once a small quarry for sand extraction. Part of the back garden included the overgrown remains of that quarry – a hole in the ground that couldn't be built on, with a little patch of remnant woodland and a small pond in the hollow. Being sandy, it was very dry, and full of lizards, butterflies, grasshoppers and crickets. I can remember that in the summer it erupted with the tall (to me at that age) spikes of self-sowing evening primroses (*Oenothera biennis*). This excavation was known as 'The Pit' by my parents, but to me it felt like a complete world of vast proportions that stretched to the horizon. In reality of course it was quite tiny, but going down into it along a winding path through rustling ripened grasses to bask in the sheltered heat of summer or catching sight of the tawny owl that lurked in the woodland patch, I felt like an intrepid explorer. In fact, at the age of about six, I gained my first inkling of the overwhelming immersive experience of nature – of feeling part of a buzzing, vibrating, multi-sensory world that was full of life, if you sat still long enough for it to come to you.

Later, when I was around the age of nine, my family moved to a village in the countryside of Kent in the south-east of England, surrounded by apple orchards, coppiced woodlands and deep lanes enclosed with over-arching hedgerows. At the little village school that I went to, we were taken out once a month on a nature walk around the lanes by Miss Whitehead, a retired teacher who came into school for the purpose. She would identity all the wildflowers we saw and give us their common names, and a bit of folklore or an interesting story about each one. For some reason, these old common names really sparked an interest in me – dog's mercury, cuckoo pint, lady's smock and so many others. Often the plants themselves might be nothing to look at, but the names and histories gave them personality and I came to know them through this. But it also got me looking at the small scale – how these individuals grew with each other, and what they seemed to like and dislike.

Top: Woodland wildflowers were my first love, their ephemeral beauty capturing my imagination. Bluebells, *Hyacinthoides non-scripta*.

Above: The dramatic foliage and seed heads of butterbur (*Petasites hybridus*) rise through a lower layer of lady's smock (*Cardamine pratensis*) in a marshy area in Derbyshire.

Once I was a little older I would go off exploring in the countryside, often cycling further afield from my home turf. I discovered the beauty of the coppiced woodlands in the spring, with exhilarating carpets of wildflowers – primroses (*Primula vulgaris*), wood anemones (*Anemone nemorosa*), violets (*Viola odorata*), wild garlic (*Allium ursinum*) and bluebells (*Hyacinthoides non-scripta*). In summer, the meadows were decorated with field scabious (*Knautia arvensis*) and greater knapweed (*Centaurea scabiosa*). I would be overwhelmed by the sheer abundance and impact of flowers stretching over large areas, but I would also embed myself in these places, be still and just soak up the atmosphere, becoming lost in the intricate detail. The earthy vegetal smells in the warm summer air of a meadow; the movement of wind through grasses; the ants or beetles jittering over the ground; the intertwining complex of foliage and stems. I could appreciate that everything worked at a variety of scales, from the miniature world of intricate interdependency that unfolded before me in my immediate field of vision and then multiplied up a thousand times or more to fill the whole field.

Opposite: Field scabious (*Knautia arvensis*) with lesser quaking grass (*Briza minor*).

In order to fully engage with the emotional experiences that I have been talking about so far, it's important to set them within some form of 'safe' frame. The 'sublime' is an 18th-century expression for highly exciting, awe-inspiring encounters with the natural world, but it was always made clear that such experiences could only be endured from a position of safety. For example, the view across a stupendous gorge with a thundering river at its base may be exhilarating when seen from a safe viewing platform, but would be much less satisfying if you'd fallen down the side of the gorge and were left hanging precariously from a rickety tree, with only the cracking tree roots making the difference between your survival or plunging to the depths!

The next level up is what I have described as legibility, or understanding, needs. Unlike the lower basic needs, these concern the detail of the actual plantings themselves – they're internal to the planting rather than external. Again, we have to go way beyond thinking that we can simply fill a space with something wild-looking. Legibility is all about clarity and making sure that it's possible to understand the key elements of the planting at a single glance. There has to be a recognizable internal organization to the planting for it to be work fully in this model: it must be structured as opposed to free-form. This might be related to plant forms, textures or colours and will involve a degree of rhythm and repetition, and it's essential to get this right for this layer in the pyramid to be satisfactory.

Top: I'm feeling quite safe and awe-struck here, enjoying the stupendous view of the Rocky Mountains from a viewing point. It would be quite a different feeling if I was looking at the same view hanging from my fingertips from a cliff-face.

Above: In a similar way, the informality of this meadow in a commercial business park setting in Sheffield is made to feel less unruly through the neat edge and heightened colour.

I've also noted the idea of 'fitness' here, and this is where ecological sensibility comes in: the sense that the vegetation is fitted to the site, is ecologically coherent within itself and with the region. In saying this, I need to emphasize that this model is intended to be suitable for someone who may have no in-depth, ecological knowledge at all. So, this isn't necessarily about having a detailed awareness of the right plants for a specific plant community. It can be a case of an intuitive sense of rightness and compatibility – a sort of inbuilt ecological wisdom. Choosing plants from similar habitats or environmental conditions often results in them having similar adaptations, and this in turn leads to a visual coherence across a planting. And it's at this level also that the essence of 'naturalness' comes in: the overall character of the planting and the arrangement of the elements to achieve the lack of rigid formality.

The factor that lifts a perfectly pleasant and effective naturalistic planting to the highest level of emotional fulfilment is the additional element of deliberate artistry. For example, it's the considered use of colour and plant forms within the naturalistic method that does it for me, and the integration of some of the more traditional aspects of planting design within the exciting spontaneity of naturalness that gives the greatest aesthetic benefit. It's not *revolution*, casting aside all that's gone before; it's *evolution*, combining the best of all worlds. A further important aspect is to move from a passive landscape or garden experience to an active one, through the concept of *immersion* – this is something we'll look at a lot more in the next sections of the book. But I've also listed the words *wonder* and *awe*. These are words of response to the sublime. And they get to the heart of the nature-enhanced idea: exaggerated effects, boldness, and being extremely rigorous in choosing the components of a planting.

Above: This steppe planting at the Barbican with its drought-tolerant grasses and forbs in shallow depths of dry soil has a sense of visual coherence through the grey and blue foliage colours of the plants. Design: Nigel Dunnett

From the Beginning

The Pictorial Meadows story

One of the first experiences I had of the potential of such planting to unlock powerful emotional reactions was through the development of Pictorial Meadows for urban applications – a process which moved from very small beginnings to reach its culmination as the backbone of the Queen Elizabeth Olympic Park for the 2012 Olympic Games in London.

I came up with the concept of Pictorial Meadows as one way of expressing the idea of 'nature-enhanced'. They are aimed at designed and disturbed sites in very urban contexts, and are intended to create a sort of meadow-max! A meadow that sings of romance, with sparkling sheets of flowers, alive with butterflies and bees, and full of exuberance; that's almost overwhelming in its beauty, and that gives a sense of working with nature, rather than against it; and that keeps on giving, over a very long period of time. It's all about creating the look and feel of a meadow – the meadow aesthetic – but in a super-charged way, based on considered use of colour, layers and structure.

Originally, these meadow mixes of annuals or perennials were developed to create reliable and dependable meadows for challenging sites – not just physically challenging, but socially too. Often they have been used on derelict and vacant plots, on 'wasteland' as a temporary filling before built development comes along, and along highway edges or central reservations. As a result, the meadows have popped up in unexpected places: residential areas and housing estates, incidental spaces, play areas – meaning that there has been a huge amount of everyday contact by people who wouldn't necessarily go out of their way to visit gardens or even parks. It's an important point – where people have no choice but to live alongside naturalistic landscapes that might have all sorts of environmental and economic benefits, these should look really good too. They need to be socially as well as environmentally sustainable.

This page: Originally, the Pictorial Meadows seed mixes were developed for urban settings like these – housing areas, derelict land, highways and parks. Seed mix design: Nigel Dunnett

Above: The Pictorial Meadows seed mixes soon became widely used by designers and home gardeners. Seed mix design: Nigel Dunnett

While I originally suspected that these flowery meadows in challenging situations would be damaged or even destroyed, I was amazed at how robust they were, and how local communities developed a real sense of ownership over them. Dogs might cause a bit of flattening here and there, and children running through might create trackways, but in my experience the meadows have the typical desire-line characteristics of short-cuts, and people tend to stick to those rather than trampling over the whole lot. What really struck me was the magnetic effect that these vibrant, colourful meadows had on people of all ages – an almost irresistible urge to get up close and experience them which is totally related to colour, and flowers, and an overwhelming abundance of them. And yes, to pick the flowers – sometimes in huge bunches. I've always been relaxed about that and see it as a sort of 'positive vandalism' – a type of contact with nature that has been all but lost to people.

The London Olympic Park Meadows

I had seen the response of people to the colourful Pictorial Meadows in a range of urban situations in Sheffield, I had written extensively about them, and they had been featured across a large number of media outlets – but nothing could have prepared me for the public reaction when these meadows became one of the centrepieces of the London Olympic Park in 2012. It was a huge honour for James Hitchmough and myself to be appointed as the principal horticultural and planting design consultants for the Olympic Park, working with the landscape architects LDA Design and Hargreaves Associates. We were taken on because John Hopkins, the head of the Olympic Park, knew about our work and wanted to make it the signature look of the park; the whole park was to be a statement about the future of horticulture and landscape design rather than a backward-looking celebration of the past.

The largest annual meadow areas in the park surrounded the main Olympic Stadium and lined the main visitor concourse. They were the first landscape elements that visitors encountered as they entered the park: pedestrian routes from car parks and rail stations went through them, and the main access bridges into the stadium went over them. It was a truly immersive experience that became a symbol for the park. The expanses of flowery meadows running for more than 1km (⅔ mile) in length were probably the first close contact that the vast majority of the six million visitors had ever had with colourful naturalistic landscape design. I designed several new colour-themed meadow mixes for the Olympic Park, including 'Olympic Gold Meadows' that shone yellow, orange and gold throughout the games period. The public response was hugely emotional; even now, many years later, people frequently mention what a lasting impression the meadows made on them. We even had to create special photography zones in the meadows so that people could have their pictures taken among the vibrant flowers.

Below: The public response to the meadows at the Olympic Park was phenomenal – for most people this would have been their first encounter with flower-rich, colourful, naturalistic designed landscapes.

Overleaf: I designed these meadow seed mixes specifically for the London Olympic Park to create the 'Olympic Gold Meadows' that surrounded the main stadium. The meadows started out orange and blue early in the summer and transformed over the weeks to rich gold and yellow.

This page: Pictorial Meadows annual flower fields at Trentham Gardens, Staffordshire. These meadows fill space beneath scattered parkland trees and flower all summer and autumn from a spring sowing. Design: Nigel Dunnett & Trentham team

Overleaf: Shimmering detail in a Pictorial Meadow at Trentham, with poppies, cornflower hybrids, white *Ammi majus*. All the green here is foliage of later flowering plants that will rise up and overtop the earlier flowerers. Design: Nigel Dunnett

Pages 42-43: One of my favourite Pictorial Meadow seed mixes is 'Pastel' which starts out with pretty pinks and whites and then by autumn makes dramatic flower fields of cosmos. Design: Nigel Dunnett

China

There has been much debate about whether the affinity we have with flowers, colour and the naturalistic experience is learned behaviour or inbuilt. I think that by now you will have realised which side of the argument I stand on! The universality of this affinity was brought home to me on a meadow-hunting trip to China. We were seeking remnants of old hay meadows in remote valleys in the region of Shangri-La in Yunnan. Just as has happened in the West, most of these old meadows have been destroyed through the drive for improvements in agricultural productivity; they have been ploughed up, drained and reseeded. But some beautiful fragments remain in inaccessible or hard-to-cultivate areas. In one such valley, surrounded by 'improved' fields of grass as far as the eye could see, a single colourful patch of meadow remained in a boggy area, full of wild primulas. Sitting in this field among the flowers were groups of local farmworkers picnicking, while their children ran around among the bright blooms. Nowhere else in the whole of the valley was this happening. It struck me that I was seeing exactly the same thing that I had come across in the housing estates and green spaces of Sheffield where Pictorial Meadows had been introduced, and here it was again, a mirror image – in physical terms thousands of miles away, but in cultural terms, a different universe.

Above and below: Farm worker families gather in a flowery meadow in rural China.

An experimental period

Because of my evolving sense of the differences between how plants grow together in the wild and the increasingly unsatisfactory way that I was seeing them used in gardens, I began to experiment with different means of arranging plants. In a way that maybe they came to regret, my parents let me play around at home with the garden, develop it and create new areas of planting. It seemed revolutionary to me at the time, but I set out a new flower bed and arranged the plants as scattered individuals, rather than in blocks or drifts, building up the whole planting like a jigsaw puzzle. It's still how I do things, but at the age of 18 or 19 it was like feeling my way in the dark towards a different way of gardening.

However, without even realizing it, the really significant thing that I started to do was to work with designed plant communities. Surrounded by the coppiced woodlands of Kent, I became fascinated by the dynamics of these managed systems: the way that hazel (*Corylus avellana*) and sweet chestnut (*Castanea sativa*) would resprout when cut to the ground and send up many new shoots; how, when the tree canopy was removed, letting in light and warmth to ground level, there was an upsurge in herbaceous plant growth – partly from buried dormant seeds, but also from permanent plants that slowly ticked over in the cool shade and were liberated into a burst of flowering energy in the new abundant light conditions. But slowly, over the years, the multi-stem trees grew taller, making more shade, until eventually a canopy was formed again, and all became subdued at ground level until the next coppicing event. This repeated cycle of light and dark, of warmth and cool, and of herbaceous and woody is actually more like a wave rising and falling over time, following a rhythm as the system develops.

And so I created my own small area of coppice. I put in small hazel trees about 1m (3¼ft) apart and underplanted them with native wildflowers such as primrose (*Primula vulgaris*), cow parsley (*Anthriscus sylvestris*), violets (*Viola odorata*) and red campion (*Silene vulgaris*). But I also threw in a few other things that I took from other parts of the garden: some colourful hybrid polyanthus (*Primula polyantha*), aquilegia (*Aquilegia vulgaris*) hybrids, sweet rocket (*Hesperis matronalis*) and honesty (*Lunaria biennis*). These were all either non-native, or cultivars of native plants, but they all suited the conditions. I then cut back the hazels every three years or so. I did all this as a way of investigating a different and more ecological way of creating and managing shrub plantings with a perennial ground cover. But inadvertently I had begun on a path that I continue with to this day: creating designed plant communities; mixing native with non-native plants that are suited to the same ecological conditions to maximize visual appeal; using different layers to extend that visual appeal over the longest time possible; and working with dynamic, ever-changing systems. Of course, at the time – the 1980s – I wouldn't have put any of it in those terms and I had no awareness that there was a movement developing across Holland and Germany that was very much in tune with my ideas.

The cut back 'stool' of a coppiced tree.

Young regrowth from a coppiced tree, with wildflowers.

North America

In the late 1980s I was very lucky to win the annual Garden Club of America/English Speaking Union Interchange Fellowship in Horticulture and spent a wonderful year and a half based at North Carolina State University, Raleigh. Ostensibly I was there to do a year's graduate study, but I actually spent most of the time travelling up and down the East Coast of the USA, visiting gardens, national parks and other natural areas. It was an exciting time for US horticulture – the so-called 'New American Garden' movement was underway, rejecting the dominance of high-maintenance European-style gardens and looking to the local landscape and plants for inspiration, embracing a more ecological way of thinking. The place for radical planting ideas was the burgeoning native plant scene, and I fell in with this in a big way.

It was the first time that I had seen so many plants that I was already familiar with from British gardens growing wild in their natural habitat. I took many road trips, many of them with my appointed supervisor, Professor J.C. Raulston, always known as JC and one of the leading US horticulturists. He was on a mission to trial and bring into cultivation new plants that were suited to the punishing climate of the south-eastern US in order to hugely extend the diversity of the cultivated landscape. JC's classes were packed out, and he was one of those academics who inspire generations of students. I took two things away from my experiences with JC and they have stayed with me ever since. First, JC saw it as his duty to make a direct link between research in the university and people in the industry, so he would spend a lot of his time working with nursery growers and landscapers in an effort to make real change. He also spoke at professional and amateur horticultural meetings all over the USA and wrote for many gardening magazines. It's something that I have tried to emulate – to share as much as possible as widely as possible, to collaborate with people who are working on the ground, and to demonstrate things rather than just talking about them.

The second ethos I got from JC was one of 'can-do'. I did an internship for a stifling humid summer at the North Carolina State University Arboretum (now the JC Raulston Arboretum) and worked alongside Edith Edelman, a garden designer and volunteer curator of the perennial border there which she had created herself. It was 100m (109yd) long and 6m (6½yd) in depth, and Edith had conceived it using Gertrude Jekyll's ideas of colour, starting with cool colours at each end and building to smouldering hot colours in the middle. But there the resemblance ended. Edith used large wild plants, bold foliage, enormous grasses – a no-holds barred expression of abandon, with none of the well-behaved and immaculately maintained perennials of the British herbaceous border that I was so used to. This was verging on anarchy – and it got even more extreme! Everything was left to stand over the winter as bleached stems and seedheads, except that Edith would spray paint over some of the standing plants to introduce colour into the darkest days. Edith had mentioned to JC the idea of making this gigantic,

Rudbeckia laciniata growing as a woodland understory along the Blue Ridge Parkway, North Carolina.

fantastical, wild cacophony of a perennial border, and his immediate response was, OK – go ahead and do it! Ever since, I've always sought the 'big idea' and have done all I can to avoid timidity, safe thinking and half-measures in garden and planting design.

Sheffield University

On returning to the UK from the US, I went on to do a PhD at the University of Sheffield. I was back into the world of pure plant ecology, studying the long-term dynamics of natural meadow vegetation. I joined the longest-running regularly monitored ecological experiment in the world – the Bibury Road Verges. These roadside grasslands in the Cotswolds had been monitored every year since 1958 as part of trials to determine the effect of different chemicals that controlled the growth of grasses as an alternative to mowing. But the 'control' plots had never received any treatments, and these were the ones I looked at. This was in the early 1990s when climate change was beginning to be talked about seriously, and the idea was that by comparing what the weather had done over the past 45 years or so with how the plants had responded to it over that time it might be possible to make predictions about the future. My PhD supervisor was Professor Phil Grime, who devised 'Plant Strategy Theory', one of world's the leading plant ecology theories. It helps to explain how plants co-exist in communities and importantly shifts the focus from thinking of plant communities as a list of individual species, to one that thinks about them consisting of different functional types. In other words, rather than considering what a plant is, it considers what a plant does. It's a very different way of looking at plant communities and it has informed my thinking greatly.

Cowslips (*Primula veris*) in the wide road verges at Bibury, Gloucestershire. For my PhD I studied the record of the long-term dynamics of plants in these verges over a 40-year period.

Regardless of the specific outcomes of that work, doing this PhD on a long-term study where the numbers and size of all the plants in permanently marked-out plots were measured every year again had a big influence on me: it taught me to take the long view, and gave me a real understanding of plant dynamics. I had to delve around endlessly in tall meadow vegetation and I got a real sense of the different layers within that grassland – what at first glance appears to be a mass of grasses and flowers is in fact vertically layered, just like a forest, but at a small scale. It also showed me how over time the actual plant composition and numbers might change a lot, but the plant community still keeps its same character and feel. From year to year, the vegetation might be quite different, depending on the weather and extreme events, but overall it remains relatively similar; I learnt not to worry about short-term fluctuations, and to accept that naturalistic plantings are ever-changing and that different plants come and go in waves, just like the coppice system I had observed earlier.

The Sheffield School

Just as I was completing my PhD in 1995, an opportunity for a lectureship came up in the Landscape Architecture Department at the University of Sheffield, teaching ecology and planting design to landscape design students. In many ways it was my dream job, so I applied and got it. By some amazing twist of fate, a year later James Hitchmough was also appointed to the department. I think that at the time we were the only two people working in the UK university sector who had similar ideas and were both equally versed in the worlds of ecology and horticulture, so it was hugely fortuitous that we both ended up at the same place, although neither of us knew each other beforehand. James had previously worked in academia in Australia then briefly in Scotland before coming to Sheffield but was already well networked into the emerging European new perennial movement, whereas I was more of a newbie to the international network. James came from a horticultural training background but had moved into ecology by practical experience, whereas I was the opposite – an ecologist by training, but a horticulturist by activity. And so we converged in the same territory, but brought different perspectives to it.

This happened at a time when conditions in the public landscape of parks and green spaces in the UK were becoming extremely difficult, with severe financial cutbacks and draining of gardening skills, and the resultant disappearance of a lot of good-quality horticulture. Together James and I worked on a wide range of different ecologically orientated planting types for parks and gardens as alternatives to the traditional highly intensive horticultural version – we developed a toolkit of options and divided up areas of focus between us, but worked to a common set of principles. What we proposed was radically different to 'urban greening' ideas that had come before, in that rather than putting ecological purity first, we focused first and foremost on how the planting looked and worked for people. Secondly, we were not tied to any rigid philosophy that native plants were always better for everything than non-native plants and freely mixed them together in our naturalistic schemes. Also, we took a different approach to the one common in the new perennial movement: we worked on the assumption that horticultural skills might not be present for detailed maintenance, and that maintenance budgets might be extremely limited. This was in marked contrast to much of the German approach, for example, which although ecological in look was actually very high-maintenance in practice, requiring a lot of knowledge.

The author with James Hitchmough.

From the Beginning

High-impact, low-input planting

In effect, we were promoting an approach to garden and landscape planting that was highly sustainable and at the same time very beautiful. The way we worked came to be known (by others) as the 'Sheffield School' of planting design; I define it as 'high-impact, low-input'. The work that we did (and still do) follows a number of guiding principles:

- To create very dramatic and beautiful visual effects, with high public appeal.
- To give year-round visual interest.
- To be very colourful and uplifting.
- To have high wildlife and biodiversity value.
- To require low-resource inputs such as water, fertilizers and time.
- To use simple, 'extensive' maintenance techniques, more similar to nature conservation than gardening – hay meadow cutting, coppicing.

Our idea was to design functioning plant communities that worked in the same way as plant communities might do in nature, but were artificial and not necessarily like anything that would ever be found in the wild. Nevertheless, they must be suited to the ecological conditions of the site. We achieved this through planting, seeding and a combination of the two.

To round off what is a rather autobiographical section, I must mention another prime influence on the way I work. One of the first things I was invited to do when I started in the Department of Landscape at the University of Sheffield was to go along on a graduate student study tour of parks and gardens in the Netherlands. One of the sites was at first glance a rather unremarkable little park in Amstelveen, a suburb of Amsterdam, with some very low-key entrances from a street in a well-to-do neighbourhood. I was unprepared for what was waiting inside: a complete world in itself of water, woodland, heathland and meadow, created from scratch on former pasture. It was here that I realized not just the power of 'created nature', but also of the importance of going beyond that and exaggerating it, thinking in a pictorial way as well as a purely ecological one.

A sown 'prairie-meadow' at RHS Wisley, Surrey.
Planting Design: James Hitchmough

CASE STUDY: THE AMSTELVEEN HEEM PARKS

The evocation of nature is, depending on your point of view, either the highest expression of the art of garden and landscape design or an uncreative sentimental pursuit that requires very little imagination. Of course, as you might expect, I sign up to the former school of thought. For me the key word here is 'evocation': putting together elements that prompt an intense emotional response in people because they convey the liberation of being in beautiful natural environments. Rather than just copying those natural models, it is a matter of enhancing their essence so that their aesthetic appeal is heightened.

A supreme and very influential example of designed nature is to be found in the neighbourhoods of Amstelveen on the outskirts of Amsterdam in the Netherlands. The parks and community spaces form an interconnected network of green, all designed on the Dutch principle of the 'Heem Park'. Heem translates as habitat or home. These started out in the 1920s as educational sites providing refuges for the wild flowers that were rapidly disappearing from the countryside as a result of changing agricultural techniques. Most towns had their own Heem Park, a community botanical garden where both schoolchildren and adults could appreciate the richness of the country's natural flora. The emphasis has changed over the years, however, and now many have come to be seen as places of great beauty instead of just educational plant collections. Nowhere is this beauty expressed more profoundly than in Amstelveen, where the

most famous of the Heem Parks is the Jac P Thijsepark. The really remarkable thing about these Amstelveen natural parks and gardens is that they are all artificial, created in the mid 20th century from agricultural land – open fields and polders. The design principles were very clear: there were to be none of the hallmarks of traditional formal design; no vistas or focal points, and the very minimum of straight lines or angles. Instead, the parks are built on the idea of mystery, using curving sinuous paths leading you on to discover what's around the corner. These paths are hugely experiential, taking you through meadows, heath and woodland and over footbridges crossing pools, waterways and ditches.

Left: Plan of the Jac P Thijssepark, showing how it wraps around the residential area with water (blue), woodland (dark purple) and meadow (light purple) areas linked by winding paths.

Above: A waterway in the park lined with alders (*Alnus glutinosa*) and underplanted with evergreen pendulous sedge (*Carex pendula*).

Pictorial planting

While the planting of the Amstelveen Heem Parks is almost exclusively native, there is very little attempt to copy wild plant communities. Instead the aim is to use wild flowers to create large-scale and uplifting plant pictures. This pictorial approach has been very influential for me, prompting the idea of Pictorial Meadows. In the spring, sheets of primrose (*Primula vulgaris*), wood anemone (*Anemone nemorosa*), fumewort (*Corydalis solida*) and many other woodland delights stretch into the distance. It's at this time that the parks are at their most dramatic, especially in April when these shady areas are at their peak.

Although these plantings are spectacular, an important principle underlying the horticultural approach was to use a majority of plants that were familiar to people and to place great emphasis on subtlety rather than attempting to create a constant and tiresome 'wow factor'. A fundamental idea was that of 'fascination': the grabbing of people's attention through the intricacies of small-scale detail.

Pond fringes are planted with great drifts of marsh marigold (*Caltha palustris*). Stands of royal fern (*Osmunda regalis*) have magnificent presence; their rapidly rising fiddleheads in the spring add bewitching drama, in summer their sheer bulk gives large-scale structure to the wetter areas and their collapsed brown foliage stays in place throughout the coldest months. Marsh spurge (*Euphorbia palustris*) is another common occupant of the wetter areas, and it grows so vigorously here that it seems to assume shrub-like character, with orange woody winter stems.

Dutch modernism

While the main snaking paths lead through the wider landscape, in places it's possible to trace more intimate trails through the plantings. These follow informal lines of square exposed aggregate concrete pavers that take you away from the main paths, over footbridges, and back to the main paths again. Garden designer Carrie Preston who lives in the Netherlands tells me that this use of modern functional materials in design is an example of Dutch modernism from the 1950s. Unlike most other parts of the world, in the Netherlands modernism in garden design and landscape architecture wasn't associated with an austere minimalist application of horticulture, and therefore these materials sit very happily with the diversity of the plantings.

Opposite top: An open glade with heathland vegetation – it's difficult to believe that these parks were created from open pasture in the twentieth century.

Opposite bottom: A dramatic 'set-piece' planting with oxlips (*Primula elatior*), violets (*Viola odorata*) and lily of the valley (*Convallaria major*) underneath a birch plantation.

Above: Royal ferns, *Osmunda regalis*, rising up in spring in bold clumps around the edge of a lake.

Left top: Winding path of modern concrete pavers through the naturalistic planting.

Left bottom: Making narrow pinch points to create a sense of moving between 'open' and 'closed' spaces is one of the characteristic features of the parks of Amstelveen.

From the Beginning

UNDERSTANDING CONTEMPORARY NATURALISM

It could be said that the whole history of garden and landscape design can be distilled into a tussle between pro- and anti-wild philosophies regarding our intimate relationship with nature. Or to put it another way: an endless tension between gardens as expressions of nature, and gardens as explicit expressions of control over nature. It's often put as the 'nature-culture' divide, and in very simple terms it's seen as a black and white choice between the formal, obviously geometric and ordered, and the informal and romantic.

Perhaps at a deeper level we can look at this as a contrast between two very different views of the natural world – one which views nature as wild, threatening, dangerous and unsafe; and another which sees it as benign, mystical and an infinite source of beauty.

CONTROLLING NATURE

The earliest gardens that we know about were very much in the former category and were enclosed areas that promoted shelter and protection, civilized values and orderly cultivation as opposed to the hostile untamed wilderness without. For example the Chinese garden tradition (more famous through the Japanese versions) is based on walled-off spaces, reserved from the external landscape, in which refined and heightened activities could occur. In content, they are highly stylized representations of ideal natural landscapes in which all the rough edges of nature are eliminated, and all is serene and simple. They are often beautiful but arguably rather sterile and safe. Similarly, in the medieval or monastic gardens of the West the *hortus conclusus* were formal walled enclosures for production or spiritual renewal that again represented civilization vs the wild nature beyond the walls – a terrifying wilderness full of evil and dangerous spirits.

Nevertheless, a common feature of the medieval garden was also the 'flowery mead' – flower-rich grass or turf areas, created by planting wild flowers and simple cultivated flowering plants at high density into existing grassland. This is very interesting in the context of this book, because it represents a sort of idealized nature – a colourful and fragrant meadowy mix, but neat, short, and with all the roughness and weeds taken out. In fact, it is a very early example of the concept of 'nature-enhanced'. It's also interesting to see the different ways in which these types of garden are depicted. The *hortus conclusus* comes across as a place of toil, with gardeners slaving away to keep the necessary order and control, while the images of the flowery mead in use seem wanton and almost decadent – people relaxing among the flowers, eating and drinking. There's a stark contrast between the almost puritanical images of production and seriousness among the rigid formal beds and the sense of unrestrained free spirits on the flowery mead, and this is remarkably similar to the ideas proposed in my modified form of Maslow's 'Hierarchy of Needs' pyramid model.

This pendulum in attitudes to nature has swung back and forth over the centuries. You might think, as a reader of this book and presumably someone who has at least a passing interest in working with gardens and landscapes in a way that is tuned to nature, that you might be immune from anti-wild thinking. But even within the field of ecologically inspired design, there's a similar contrast in attitudes. There's 'good nature', well-structured, diverse, understandable and attractive; and there's 'bad nature', weedy, messy, low-diversity. When it comes down to it, the idea of Nature is all in the mind.

This is not the place for an extended foray into garden design history, but there are two movements that I think are very relevant to current views on what makes or doesn't make 'good' designed nature and what lies at the core of the emotional response to nature that is the cornerstone of this book. It's worth taking a brief look at them, because they have largely guided us to the point at which we are now.

Throughout garden history there has been a long tradition of formal geometry, straight lines, angles, vistas and focal points, and tight control as seen here at Gravetye Manor (above), Pitmedden (opposite below) and Trentham (previous page).

Opposite above: The eighteenth-century Capability Brown parkland at Chatsworth House represents a much more informal and 'natural' tradition, but in its own way is equally contrived.

The Picturesque

The old cliché that there is nothing new under the sun is definitely true of the discussions and arguments that gave rise to the Picturesque idea. It came to prominence at the end of the 18th-century English landscape movement, when the dominance of Capability Brown-style natural scenes as the overriding aesthetic started to ebb. These discussions and arguments were vigorous indeed and concerned the very meaning of what nature was in relation to garden and landscape design, how best to represent it, and what constituted 'good taste' in the making of gardens that represented nature. I once spent an engrossing summer in libraries, delving in great detail into the original documents from the time, and was struck by how similar the points made then were to the same sort of discussions that we have now – except that today many would be had over social media. By contrast, learned gentlemen at the end of the 18th century wrote in elegant long-hand to each other, even resorting to poetry. But the backwards and forwards, response and counter-response were just as lively, personal, and at times vindictive, as anything to be found online in the present day.

Key players included Humphrey Repton, William Gilpin, Uvedale Price and Richard Payne Knight. They challenged the idea that the idealized Brownian landscape with its pastures, sinuous lakes and clumps of trees and woodland was in anyway natural and instead characterized it as bland, sanitized, boring, safe, simplistic and controlled. Instead, they proposed that nature was rough, irregular, wild, challenging, unpredictable and emotionally exciting. Indeed the original catalyst for these ideas was Edmund Burke's 1757 publication *A Philosophical Enquiry into the Origin of Our Ideas of the Sublime and Beautiful*, which posited a scale of emotional response to landscapes from the comfortable unthreatening feelings engendered by 'beautiful' landscapes of gentle forms and curves (the typical Capability Brown English landscape style) through to the extreme emotions of fear, terror and awe caused by 'sublime' landscapes of raw nature – treacherous mountains, crashing waterfalls, dark impenetrable forests. The term 'Picturesque' was introduced as a halfway point – rough, irregular nature but in a non-threatening context – a sort of picture-book, romantic view of attractive wildness. This was throughout a male discussion and it is no surprise that the outcomes were highly gendered: 'Beauty' was gentle and curvaceous, 'Picturesque' and 'Sublime' rugged and adventurous. But the point is that these attitudes still shape much thinking in naturalistic planting design today.

This page: Hackfall, North Yorkshire, is a classic picturesque garden, with a dramatic and awe-inspiring valley setting, ruined buildings, and complete with artificial castle – a romantic view of wild nature that is, in reality, highly crafted and staged.

There are two elements to this – one helpful to the philosophy of this book, and the other very unhelpful. The former is the idea that a Picturesque landscape, garden or planting is based, by definition, on the making and framing of attractive 'pictures' of nature. In other words, it's a composition that requires artistic skill and is very obviously contrived – something put together for pictorial effect, with imperfections eliminated, rather than trying to slavishly copy a natural scene, habitat or plant community. This pictorial view of nature – one that I tend to work with – is what separates the horticulturist, gardener or designer from the ecologist, restorationist or nature conservationist.

However, the latter is that in the original Picturesque visions, nature was seen as something that comes in once the controlling hand of people is taken away, so a lot of Picturesque ideas are related to a romantic sense of decay and neglect: of tumbledown ruins colonized by the encroaching wild, and a fascination for the small-scale irregular details of the natural world. As a result, the Picturesque idea came to be associated with a rustic and sentimental way of thinking and working; a focus on fussy small-scale details, and a celebration of the rural, the past, and quaint landscapes in slight decay. It's still with us today as the basis for much of what is done in horticulture and garden design. You only have to go to the Chelsea Flower Show to see, year after year, Picturesque and rustic displays of naturalistic plantings teamed with charming, 'dilapidated' artisan buildings. It's that combination of romanticism and sentimentality that seems to be strongly associated with the natural look. Certainly, this viewpoint has very little to say to forward-looking ideas or contexts, or to urban living, and it's a fundamental principle with me that I should avoid falling into that rustic sentimental trap.

It's worth noting in passing that the 'sublime' in landscape is an idea that is well worth revisiting. I'd say that much of what I do is about creating 'sublime' landscape and garden experiences. The idea of only being able to properly appreciate the power of such experiences if you are grounded in a sense of safety and security takes us right back again to that modified Maslow's triangle.

Modernism

If the Picturesque idea of nature took root because of its innate appeal to popular and romantic sentiment, then the modernism of the mid-20th century sought to purge that sentimentality from landscape and thinking altogether, to produce a pure, cleansed vision based on logic, science and rational thinking. Any sense of the rustic was eliminated, and attempts to copy nature in all its small-scale detail and intricacy were discounted as fussy and muddled. Modernist thinking was tuned to urban living, and looked to a bright technological future. The randomness and chaos of nature was swapped for simple clean lines and a strong sense of order, and minimalism tended to be the guiding principle in terms of planting design. Indeed there was a clear perception that creating natural-looking landscapes (the ideal of many nature-inspired designers being that the end result should appear to have not been designed at all) was not actually true design and didn't require much creative skill. Unfortunately, this impression that ecological thinking and design creativity don't go hand in hand still persists to this day.

Alongside the rather puritan approach of modernism stands a rich exploration of abstract organic forms as a basis for this ordered style. Perhaps the best-known examples are the gardens of North American landscape designer Thomas Church as espoused in his classic 1955 work *Gardens are for People*. These gardens and others featured beautiful curving amoebic shapes for lawns, pools and planted areas that all interlocked in a highly satisfying manner and produced a strong sense of unity and coherence.

It might seem strange to include mention of modernism here because at first glance it would seem to go against much of what is thought to be special in naturalistic planting design. But the cleansing of sentimental thinking and the elimination of the twee, folksy and rustic tendencies that have bedevilled a lot of ecological-leaning design practice is essential in making planting that is tuned to nature into a progressive force that is equally at home in the crowded modern city as it is in the country estate – for example the 'Dutch modernism' style of using simple concrete pavers among naturalistic plantings as opposed to rustic or natural materials. The elimination of fussiness and over-reliance on small-scale detail in favour of clarity and big-picture thinking is another important lesson. And finally, ruthless selection of elements (for example plants that can justify their inclusion only through form or function, rather than purely to promote diversity) is a guiding point.

Strange as it may seem, both romantic Picturesque ideas and clinical objective modernism have both been highly influential in shaping what we now consider to be some of the main elements of contemporary naturalism.

Above: In its modest way, this use of square concrete aggregate pavers in the Jac P Thijssepark in Amstelveen makes its own modernist statement among the naturalistic planting.

THREE STRANDS IN CONTEMPORARY NATURALISM

The terms 'naturalistic planting design' and 'new perennial planting' are thrown around a lot and the assumption is that they describe the same thing and that we all understand it. But the reality is that contemporary naturalism is purely an umbrella term. And it is an enormous and very wide umbrella that covers a very diverse range of approaches and strands.

Each of these approaches has its own design terminology and methodology, and its own way of representing the arrangement of plants. Some of these approaches can be very technical, some are very complex, and the sheer array of what constitutes 'naturalistic' can be very confusing. In this book I hope to make sense of this confusion and complexity, and to propose a set of common principles and concepts that form the basis of a naturalistic planting design methodology.

So, after the brief contextual and historical interlude, let's return to the idea of making sense of contemporary naturalism, and explore how the divergence in thinking between the Picturesque and modernism might have influenced this diversity.

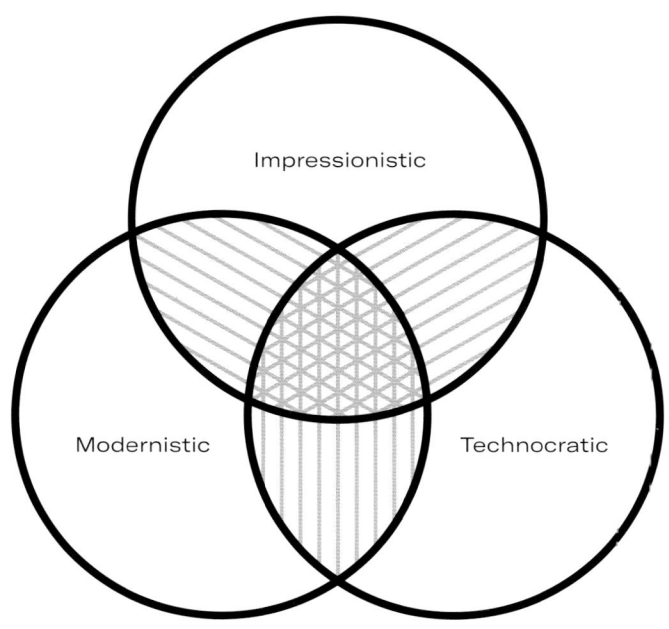

It's possible to identify three strands within naturalism, all of which have their merits and distinctive points. Of course there's a lot of overlap between the strands, but this allows us to establish the main differences between them. I call the three strands a) Impressionistic naturalism b) Technocratic naturalism and c) Modernistic naturalism. Each has its own merits and I like to pull together what I consider to be the best elements of each.

Impressionistic naturalism

By far the oldest of the three strands, this is deeply embedded in 20th-century planting design and could be said to be a direct descendent of the romantic Picturesque idea. It's where our modern ideas of the 'wild garden' had their gestation, and where horticulture and art began to come together to regard plant cultivation in gardens and landscapes as being less about the growing of individual specimens and more about plants as elements in a composition. It's where we get the first inklings of ecological ideas (even though the science of ecology hadn't been invented yet) in William Robinson's *The Wild Garden* (1870), in which he proposed the naturalization of hardy perennials into existing habitats of meadow, woodland and wetland. It epitomizes the 'right plant, right place' idea, in which plants are grown in conditions that match their natural habitats. But it also kick-started a somewhat controversial idea that I continue to work with – that of 'enhanced nature', pepping up what might otherwise seem to be somewhat low-key vegetations for designed landscapes with the addition of extra species for heightened drama or extended display. And Robinson also played an important role in popularizing a growing movement that reacted against formality, excess and artificiality in favour of a much more relaxed approach inspired by the patterns in nature.

The person we really need to concentrate on here, though, is Gertrude Jekyll (1843–1932). This might seem a strange statement when a lot of radical contemporary naturalistic designers would say that she stands for everything that they are against. Yes, Jekyll did work in a much more rigid way than we would propose now, with clearly defined drifts and blocks of the same species and shorter species at the front of a planted area, building tier-like to the tallest at the back – but as an artist herself, who was enthralled by the works of the Impressionists, she brought ideas about colour and light into the horticulture-dominated world of garden planting. And although she is best known for relatively formal flower borders, she was heavily influenced by William Robinson and her writings are suffused with her inspiration from the copses, woodlands, heathlands and meadows that surrounded her home, Munstead Wood. Here's a paragraph from *Wood and Garden* (1899) to give a flavour:

> Marshy hollows in the valleys are brilliant with Marsh Marigold (*Caltha palustris*); damp meadows have them in plenty; but they are largest and handsomest in the alder-swamps of our valley bottoms where their great luscious clumps rise out of pools of black mud and water.

Opposite and left: Painterly, impressionistic, informal planting in the Arts and Crafts tradition, using bold groupings of individual species and cultivars, let loose in dramatic abandon. Sleightholmedale Lodge, North Yorkshire. Design: Rosanna James

She incorporated elements from that surrounding landscape in her garden, for example the sandy heathlands of birch, juniper and Scotch rose (*Rosa spinosissima*) were a frequent reference. But both Robinson and Jekyll were integral to the Arts and Crafts movement, and as a result further reinforced the rustic and artisanal association of naturalistic planting with a romantic and sentimental view of rural life, traditional crafts and cottage-garden muddle.

However, it's Jekyll's link to Impressionism that is the crucial thing here, and the treatment of plants as an artistic medium, using them in a way akin to the brush strokes in an Impressionist painting to build an abstract composition that is highly informed by colour relationships. It's often referred to as a painterly method of planting design, but it's also a highly pictorial one that has epitomized much of British garden design for the past hundred years.

A key element in putting together such compositions is the concept of *plant association*. This is the skilful placing of plants in combination to create harmonious or contrasting visual effects based on form, colour and texture. It's the basis of the standard detailed planting plan, whereby individual plants or groups of plants are placed next to each other in a very studied and precise way. It's where a lot of creativity and artistry comes into working with plants, and although designers use a plan to do this, gardeners and garden-makers will be much more hands-on, physically moving plants around to achieve satisfying combinations.

Right: The art of plant association. In the top picture, form, colour and texture of individual plants are combined into pleasing groupings at Great Dixter and in the bottom picture, groups of plants with the same rounded forms, but with different textures and colours, are used to flank a path at RHS Wisley, Surrey in a planting design by Tom Stuart-Smith.

Understanding Contemporary Naturalism

It's important to understand the centrality of deliberately combining plants to achieve the desired outcome, whether this be as individuals or in groups, blocks or drifts. For me, it is important because it enables precise outcomes to be achieved in a way that other methods might not. This is particularly so when working with colour. The other two naturalistic planting strands rely much less on deliberate plant association, and as we shall see, the idea of working with traditional colour theories or ideas is seen as very regressive. However, I disagree: my feeling is that if colour is thought about in detail alongside other principles of naturalistic planting, then it can lift the design to a whole different level. But of course the deliberate and artful combination of plants lacking a primary focus on ecological compatability and dynamics can require both a huge amount of skill to generate a truly spontaneous and naturalistic effect, followed by intensive and highly skilled maintenance to maintain that illusion.

Current designers who continue this impressionistic and highly artful tradition and skilfully combine it with a contemporary ecological sensibility include Dan Pearson, Tom Stuart-Smith and Sarah Price.

Top: The Courtyard in Tom Stuart-Smith's private garden.

Above: The Italian Garden, Trentham. Planting Design: Tom Stuart-Smith

Understanding Contemporary Naturalism

Technocratic naturalism

Whereas the impressionistic strand of naturalism is based on artistic and studied plant combinations and associations, observing the wild as an amateur natural historian might, the technocratic strand is very different, being much more scientific and technical in its methodology. As a result, it's more akin to modernist thinking than Picturesque in its rejection of the rules of the past and its distinct non-rustic attitude.

In simple terms, the technocratic strand is most clearly associated with the German tradition in contemporary naturalistic planting design, which had wide international influence following the publication of the classic *Perennials and their Garden Habitats* by Richard Hansen and Freidrich Stahl (Timber Press, 1993). However, this was but the latest expression of a much longer tradition of using wild perennials in bold ways, with a naturalistic arrangement kicked off by the work of Karl Foerster and others in the 1920s and '30s (see modernistic naturalism page 66). But Hansen and Stahl, and the burgeoning use of naturalistic perennial planting in public spaces and garden festivals in Germany in the 1980s and '90s, brought this concept to a much wider audience outside Germany and applied a rigorous scientific conceptual framework to it.

The technocratic approach is best seen as the integration of scientific ecological principles with the horticultural practice of growing plants in designed and cultivated contexts – horticultural ecology if you like, or ecological horticulture. Rather than amateur observation of plants or plant communities in the wild, technocratic naturalism is based upon detailed scientific measurement and recording, experimental trials, and a lot of classification of plants into different ecological types to help inform design. That classification might be related to growth form and habit; competitiveness; the relative tendency of plants to grow as single isolated individuals through to vigorous clonal masses (plant sociability); or the types of natural habitat that they come from.

There's a tendency within this strand to develop relatively strict planting design rules and methodologies, some of which can be overwhelmingly complex. For example, Hansen and Stahl worked with a terminology of 'specimen or structural plants' (which form the main framework for the planting); 'theme plants' (which form the main visual impression at any one time); 'companion plants or groundcovers' (which support the main visual displays) and 'filler plants' (seasonal plants such as bulbs or annuals that create short seasonal highlights). Plantings were designed as a set of layers, with the distributions of each of these types of plants, starting with the structural plants and ending with the fillers. This design methodology was reimagined and made available to a whole new audience in Thomas Rainer and Claudia West's ground-breaking book *Planting in a Post-Wild World* (Timber Press, 2015). However, many of these rules have been based on a fairly narrow range of plant community types and are by no means the end of the story, and should not necessarily be seen as the only way to work. For example, the meadow community that we look at in detail in the next chapter offers huge scope for further exploration of other natural models.

Much technocratic naturalism could be described as biogeographic, in that it works with plant communities from different parts of the world (for example prairie and steppe) and creates designed versions of these plant communities, working with species that tend to come from the same geographic area (even if the actual planting is in a completely different country or region).

Top and above: This roof terrace at Moorgate Crofts Business Centre, Rotherham, South Yorkshire was planted using the 'random planting' method, without a detailed planting plan. Planting Design: Nigel Dunnett

Technocratic naturalist planting plans are fiendishly difficult and time-consuming to interpret and this is one of the reasons why the current idea of random planting has come to such prominence. This holds that to achieve a truly spontaneous and naturalistic effect there is no need to consider the placing of individual plants. Instead, plant mixes are composed of species carefully chosen to be compatible with each other under specified ecological conditions, with different proportions of the species, and these are then planted randomly throughout the defined area. While much of the focus has been on mixes created through the use of container-grown plants by designers such as Cassian Schmidt, exactly the same principles apply to the use of seed mixes, as comprehensively explained by my colleague James Hitchmough in his 2017 book *Sowing Beauty*. Both plant and seed mixes tend to be the result of extensive scientific work carried out by, or in association with, university researchers.

The key things to note about the technocratic approach are the primacy of ecological compatibility as a main driver for plant selection, and the use of 'reference' natural or semi-natural plant communities as the basis for designed versions of these communities. The use of random planting techniques removes any essence of 'plant association' beyond that contained in the original mixture, and any detailed placing of plants is not possible. The results can be truly amazing, with a feel of energy and spontaneity, and the scientific foundation gives a sense of reliability.

Further, the focus on making designed plant communities means that some of the more 'artful' elements of planting design are not considered to be useful in this context and are not really a consideration – it's more about putting plants together that are ecologically suited and compatible, rather than using the more traditional ideas of colour theory, for example. Indeed, many would argue that these traditional ideas are irrelevant when dealing with an 'ecological aesthetic' which is bound by completely different rules and principles. In this context, the approach is modernist in that it consciously reacts against received wisdoms, hasn't got a trace of tweeness about it, and is not concerned with small, intricate details of individual plant combinations for picturesque effect, instead aiming for a purity of outcomes, achieved in the most efficient manner. But because the emphasis is on the designed plant community, there is a tendency to fill large spaces with the same thing, and there may be difficulty in applying the ideas to smaller areas. The primary driving force of ecological compatibility for plant selection can also result in a visual mish-mash of incompatible forms and colours, depending on your viewpoint.

Much of my own work of and that of James Hitchmough in the Sheffield School could be said to fall broadly into this technocratic category.

Above: The Fantasticology area at the Queen Elizabeth Olympic Park, London was created from a designed seed mix. Planting Design: Nigel Dunnett

Above right: The prairie meadow at RHS Wisley, Surrey was created from a designed seed mix. Planting Design: James Hitchmough

Opposite: This perennial meadow at Trentham Gardens, Staffordshire was also set out by the random planting method which can produce very spontaneous, naturalistic effects, seen here in late spring and autumn. Planting Design: Nigel Dunnett

Modernistic naturalism

I've noted before the purging effect of modernism in removing clutter and unnecessary decorative ornamentation in favour of clarity, simplicity and rigorous selection of elements to maximize function and efficiency. There can be a temptation in naturalistic planting to celebrate high species diversity and the wild look. A similar rigorous selection of elements and simplicity of form is one way to overcome the natural tendency for diverse naturalistic plantings to deteriorate into untidiness. The old adage that beauty is in the eye of the beholder comes into play here. Appreciation of the ecological look can be a learnt response – those in the know naturally assume that everyone shares the same viewpoint, but one person's celebration of ecological diversity and structural layering can be another person's unholy mess.

Piet Oudolf, the designer who has done more than anyone else to popularize the contemporary naturalistic look, works within a more structured framework than is apparent in the other two strands. Piet has been heavily influenced by what could be termed 'Dutch modernism', expressed most clearly in the work of the famous landscape and garden architect Mien Ruys (1904–99). In the same way that the Arts and Crafts designers combined geometric architectural garden layouts with loose impressionistic planting, Ruys teamed strong and simple layouts with loose and relaxed planting. But the styles could not be more different; while the Arts and Crafts ideal was rustic and traditional, using natural hand-crafted materials, the modernist approach was to use modern industrial materials and abstract as well as formal geometry. Whereas most modernist garden designers saw any sort of horticultural non-woody intricate planting as unnecessary frivolous froth, Ruys embraced the spark of dynamic perennial planting and layered it into her architectural frameworks – but however loose the planting might be, she kept to a clear mantra of simplicity and clarity.

Opposite and top: Piet Oudolf's main planting style is defined by the use of bold structural perennials that look as good in winter as they do in summer. Summer and autumn photos taken at Trentham Gardens, Staffordshire.

Above: Naturalistic planting in an uncompromising modern and urban setting, The Lurie Garden, Chicago. Planting Design: Piet Oudolf

Right: Bold and dramatic planting: the river of grass at Trentham in autumn with mass planting of *Molinia caerulea* cultivars. Planting Design: Piet Oudolf

Ruys's planting influences were radical: the bold and free use of perennials and ornamental grasses that had developed in Germany, with nurseryman and designer Karl Foerster (1874–1970) and others rigorously selecting plants for garden hardiness, reliability and ease of maintenance, with a focus on year-round structure and form. Flowering perennials were used in large informal masses, punctuated with upright and structural grasses and perennials. Like Gertrude Jekyll, Foerster was influenced by the wild garden ideas of William Robinson, but she took off in a different direction from the painterly approach of the Impressionists to embrace bold, radical plant arrangements that made dramatic impact.

While in Germany this led on to the scientific technocratic strand of naturalism, in the Netherlands it went off into a different, softer direction that, as well as ecological functionality, had more room for aesthetic considerations and elements of considered plant association rather than random combinations. The example of the Heem Parks of Amstelveen has already been given: seemingly natural parks and gardens, but with a strong and clear overall design, bold groupings and sweeps of wildflowers, and with modern hard landscape materials.

In the work of Piet Oudolf we see many elements of this softened modernism and relatively little of the impressionistic or Picturesque thinking. So, there is a very rigorous approach to plant selection, with focus on form, structure and function rather than floral decoration. Earlier Oudolf plantings tended to be based on relatively simple interlocking drifts and blocks of perennials and grasses, with an overlying more random arrangement of emergent or structural perennials and grasses. Later plantings are more mingled or mixed, but even here there is a simple and clear structure, with individual mixes themselves being arranged in sweeps and drifts. And the individual mixes are simple, composed of small numbers of carefully chosen species. This is a far cry from the diverse random mixing of the technocratic strand.

Above: Matrix planting with sweeps of grasses and emergent perennials and multi-stem trees. Hauser and Wirth, Somerset. Planting Design: Piet Oudolf

Above: Loose and informal planting, with clean modern shapes. Hauser and Wirth, Somerset. Design: Piet Oudolf

In the USA, the new American garden movement of the 1980s, spearheaded by Wolfgang Oehme and James van Sweden, similarly used big, incredibly bold mass groupings of layered perennials and grasses in a clearly modernist way, but it was promoted as a naturalistic alternative to the dominant European garden style prevalent in the USA, and one which was much more in tune with the grandeur and scale of the American landscape. The highly respected American landscape architect Darrel Morrison, although walking in the picturesque shoes of Jens Jensen, uses native species in highly stylized and abstracted plant communities that are distilled into their key character species, arranged in simple mixes laid out in flowing drifts in a clean modernistic style.

The clarity of form and simplicity of organization gives this modernist strand one clear advantage: legibility. In other words it has order and form, and is relatively straightforward to understand, compared to the free-form randomness of the technocratic strand. In its rigorous plant selection, promotion of plant form over floral embellishment and lack of sentimentality, it is perfectly suited to modern and highly urban environments as well as rural ones. The focus on simple mixes and combinations of plants makes for much greater possibility for artfulness and studied aesthetics. But the exuberance and abandon of the spontaneous technocratic strand can be absent, and the relentless focus on form and function can, like modernism itself, be rather lacking in warmth and emotional soul.

Summary of the three strands in contemporary Naturalistic Planting Design

Type	Impressionistic	Technocratic	Modernistic
Core attribute	Painterly, artful	Scientific	Abstract
Main method	Plant association	Plant mixes	Plant mixes, plant association
Key driver for plant choice	Colour	Ecological plant community	Plant form
Arrangement	Drifts and blocks	Complex interactions, layers	Drifts, complex interactions

THE WAY FORWARD

The three strands each have benefits and disadvantages, but navigating your way between them and trying to make sense of the different terminologies and design methodologies can be highly confusing. In this book, I propose a road map through all of these which brings together the best of all, and presents a simple set of principles and ways of thinking that will help to create structured, immersive gardens and landscapes that work at the human scale. I call it the Universal FLOW model for planting design.

This fills the black spot at the intersection between these different strands, and the key characteristic for me is that it reintroduces the idea of plant association to the language of naturalistic planting design and brings a much-needed element of considered artfulness into the scientific rigour and randomness of the technocratic approach.

But before we get to the detail of the method, we need to take a step back and embark on an immersive visual tour of the world of nature, look in some depth at inspiring and uplifting examples, pull out some key ideas and lessons, and then think about how we can apply them to make equally inspiring and uplifting designed plantings of our own.

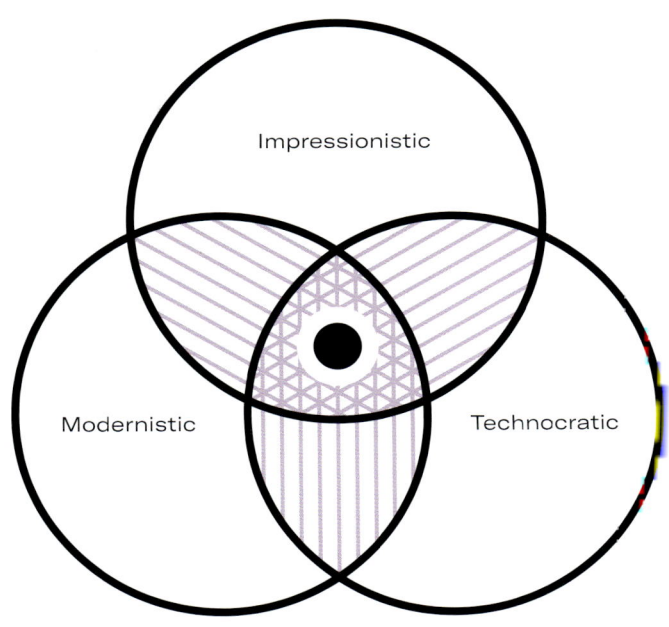

Left: This is part of a much larger planting scheme by the author at the Barbican, London and is the result of a great deal of background science, research, and trials. It has a dramatic visual character, full of contrast in textures and forms and is multi-layered. It has a strongly naturalistic character, and plants are used in intimate associations, and yet it is relatively simple and abstract. There is a large element of randomness in terms of how the plants are arranged, but this is within a strong framework of deliberately placed structural plants. It's an example of a synthesis of impressionistic, scientific and modernistic approaches to naturalistic planting design.

READING NATURE

Many people will say that they are 'inspired by nature', but what does that really mean? Are we all talking about the same thing, and do we have the same reference points? In this section I shall explain my own set of inspirations and reference points. I have come to it over time and it's purely personal – although I hope it is shared by many others – and is based on a lot of experience. From making observations and developing this set of principles, I've established my own rule book for structuring, designing and planting landscapes, gardens, or areas of gardens that capture the essence and emotional power of beautiful natural landscapes but have that exaggerated, enhanced quality that I outlined in the first chapter. In this chapter, I shall set out the basis for that rule book. I'll be doing it in a mostly visual way, using a set of images to draw out some key points that we'll then apply in a 'planting design methodology'.

NATURAL PLANT COMMUNITIES

It's essential to become familiar with inspiring examples of natural plant communities. This doesn't mean that you have to travel to remote places to study amazing plant communities in their natural habitat – after all, my own fascination with nature began in my own childhood back yard, and with the lanes, hedgerows and woodlands around where I lived. I'm equally enchanted by the intricate, intimate experience of clusters of wild plants huddling round the base of a tree, or with the loose combinations of meadow flowers and wild grasses in a patch of unmown grass, or naturalized plants springing up on the edges of an urban brownfield site. In fact, urban areas are full of inspiration – you don't need to go on a rural expedition. But the point is that there is nothing to beat first-hand experience of observing the interactions of plants in a plant community. And this needs to be done over time – it's only by watching the same area long-term that any sense of the dynamics of plant communities can be gained. I can't over-emphasize that an understanding of change over time is crucial.

This sense of familiarity and developing a feeling for natural interactions within plant communities can be combined with extensive virtual research to identify inspirational natural plant communities from around the world and explore their character, form and structure. You can, if you wish, undertake in-depth research into the component plant species and develop your own versions of these communities, using the 'bio-geographic' approach but I don't believe this is essential. What is more vital is to get a visual sense of the ecology, patterning and processes going on in those inspirational examples and to identify what it is that excites you about them. That's why I emphasize the importance of a visual ecology as the basis for planting design that's tuned to nature, rather than a taxonomic ecology. It liberates us from the straitjacket of taxonomic lists. There's nothing

Above: Patches of beautiful nature are all around us: a churchyard in rural Suffolk.

Below: Spontaneous vegetation on an old industrial site in Duisburg, Germany.

wrong with those, but why lose out on the creative and artful possibilities of going beyond what might occur purely by chance in nature? One only has to look at the 'recombinant' or 'novel' plant communities that come together on abandoned urban sites, comprising both native and non-native plant species, to know that there is no magic to the fact that plant combinations in the wild might have existed for millennia. In fact, these 'recombinant' communities – the sort of 'future nature' that I've referred to before – represent for me the best model for creating new designed plant communities. The arguments for and against native plant use have been well-rehearsed and there's no need to go into them in depth here. Suffice to say that I instinctively swerve away from any discussions where the options are presented in stark binary terms, and you believe either in the complete righteous truth or nothing at all. I work with native plants and plant communities all the time – they're often my starting point – but I do it for ethical reasons, and because they fit visually, rather than because of scientific principle. I believe that if we work responsibly and take an aesthetic viewpoint first and foremost with naturalistic plantings in designed settings, we'll create huge pleasure for people and there will be plenty of wider ecological benefit.

Top: Spontaneous urban colonizing plants growing on brick rubble at a demolition site in Sheffield with red valerian (*Centranthus ruber*) and oxeye daisy (*Leucanthemum vulgare*).

Above: Naturalized North American asters on an abandoned site in Sheffield.

Rather than skimming through a wide range of different landscapes and climatic zones for inspiration, I'm going to look in depth at just one main landscape, and mostly at a few sites within that landscape, although I'll address some others along the way. In so doing I think it's easier to draw out a set of principles that can be applied on a wide basis, adapted to whatever climate zone or landscape context you are working in.

Above: Although most people would describe this as a 'natural' landscape in the north of England, there is in fact nothing here that has not been altered, changed or managed by people.

Opposite: This abandoned old field in Pennsylvania, USA, is becoming colonized by *Liquidambar styraciflua* trees. There's a very clear structure here, with the trees forming the 'walls' that enclose an open glade with a 'floor' of grasses including the pennisetum in the foreground. The photo was taken from one 'room' looking into another. In a few more years the trees will have grown high enough to form an overhead canopy or 'ceiling'.

Natural or semi-natural?

Let's start by looking at some of the ways in which plants arrange themselves in natural plant communities. Because much of my own inspiration comes from meadow-like, flower-rich landscapes, I'll devote some time to analysing some particularly striking examples of these.

First, I want to make a note about the word 'natural', which I'll use throughout this section. What I actually mean here is non-designed plant communities. Most of what I'll be concerned with is not natural at all, in the sense that it is the result of some form of management, usually agricultural, such as grazing –so really it should be called semi-natural. But the crucial point is that nothing I discuss in this section has actually been designed to look the way it does – it's the result of natural and ecological processes operating within the context of whatever sort of human influence might be occurring in that landscape.

THE BUILDING BLOCKS OF LANDSCAPE

I'm going to consider naturalistic landscape in the same way that an architect might contemplate a building or settlement, rather than look it at from the point of view of a botanist, ecologist or horticulturist. In other words, I'll forget about the individual plants or combinations of plants, and concentrate instead on its structure – the 'walls', 'floors', and 'ceilings' of the landscape, how they form the individual rooms or spaces, how they are connected together, and how they combine to make a larger whole. The idea of the 'outdoor room' is nothing new in garden design, of course, but often this is related more to thinking about functions and contents. Here I'm addressing how to make the rooms in the first place!

I find this is a very useful way of thinking. It enables me to work with structural types of vegetation, rather than getting bogged down at the outset with long lists of species. I think of them as building blocks which can be used in different combinations to construct the sort of designed landscape or garden experience through planting that I'm aiming for. There's more about this in the next chapter. But for now, I'll start at a very simple level and consider the floor plan layer as being composed of the herbaceous layers in a landscape; of the wall layer as being shrub-based and edge; and of the ceiling layer being tree-based and forest.

FLOOR PLAN

The floor plan is the horizontal plane in the landscape, and in terms of human scale, it's the one that we view at the same sort of level as ourselves. It's the one constant, running in different forms through the wall and ceiling layers. It largely refers to the herbaceous layer in a landscape, although by no means exclusively so. When I refer to the floor layer or floor plan, I'm really referring to the idea of filling space with planting: the contents of any particular space, large or small, that is defined by some sort of edge or division from another area of floor planting. That edge or division can be just slightly taller than the main floor area, or have a markedly different form or texture – it doesn't have to be a strong physical barrier.

Examples of floor layer plant communities

The idea of 'reference' plant communities is an important one in naturalistic planting design. These are natural or semi-natural plant communities that provide an inspirational starting point for creating designed versions. Specific reference points for the 'floor plan' include:

- Grassland types: prairie, steppe, pampas, meadow. Of course, within these categories are myriad different variants according to how wet/dry, warm/cool and so forth the environment is.

- Low shrub: heathland, tundra, low scrubland.

- Wetland types: open water (still or moving); marsh (salt and fresh); marginal vegetation.

Top: Wild blue phlox, *Phlox divaricata*, carpets a woodland meadow in Illinois, USA. This is an example of the floor layer occurring beneath other layers. Indeed, the meadow is bounded by 'walls' of shrubs around the edge, and the tall canopy trees create a 'ceiling' to this landscape.

Above: The floor layer does not have to be short, heights are all relative, it's more about the dominant vegetation that fills a space. Here, thin-leaved sunflower, *Helianthus decapetalus*, is flowering in a wet meadow/prairie that fills a river flood plain in Illinois, USA.

Left: A beautiful area of steppe grassland in Ukraine. Purple *Salvia nemorosa* flowers among the graceful flowers of feather grass, *Stipa pennata*. The deeper green areas are masses of lady's bedstraw, *Galium verum*, which will soon be flowering with golden yellow clusters of fragrant flowers.

Opposite: Examples of floor-level vegetation types from meadow and grassland (top) to low-shrub (middle) and wetland (bottom) types.

THE WALLS

Landscapes composed of only 'floor plan' vegetation are wide-open and vast. Impressive at first, but soon becoming visually overwhelming, and without anything to break them up, leading to lack of legibility and understanding. We begin to feel lost and small. We need a degree of 'structure' in a landscape to help us feel at home. It brings us back to the idea of 'prospect and refuge' that we looked at earlier. By 'walls' in the natural landscape I mean anything that could be said to frame a space, or that creates permanent structure within a space. Like human-built walls, these may be of any size or height; they may be solid or transparent, dense or open, continuous or staggered or merely the faintest suggestion of a structure. And generally, for a sense of permanence and robustness, these 'walls' will include woody plants as well as herbaceous or perennial plants.

The role of woody vegetation in forming the 'walls' in a natural landscape, defining spaces and giving them punctuation varies according to the height and complexity of that vegetation. The degree of enclosure and the feeling of space may be related to the height of the vegetation compared to the height of the human body. Therefore, working on the idea of intimate space, and thinking at the human scale, it is useful to subdivide these structural forms into two main categories very simply by height: shrubs and trees. While the true definition of a shrub is that it is a multi-stemmed woody plant as opposed to a single-stemmed tree, to me shrubs are generally of a human scale and size as opposed to trees, which clearly are bigger. That simple definition suits our purpose here because shrub-based natural landscapes are completely different to woodlands and forests, largely because of how they relate to people in terms of scale. They've also been hugely neglected as a model for planting design, so we'll start with them.

There's a huge range of inspiring shrub-dominated vegetation types, many of which are very familiar. We can use them as 'reference' plant communities in exactly the same way that perennial or grassland communities have been used for many years. The generic terms of 'shrublands' (or scrub or brush) refers to plant communities composed mostly of shrubs, although they will often include grasses, herbs, small trees and bulbs. The Mediterranean maquis, the chaparral of California, the South African fynbos and different types of heathland are all examples. Some of these types might be called 'closed shrub', in that they have a dense foliage cover and form dense thickets, while others are more 'open', with the shrub component more scattered or clumped.

Right, above: Mixed scrub with berberis, willows, rhododendrons, wild roses, enclosing pockets of grassland: floor plan and walls.

Right, below: Calcareous scrubland, central Europe, with privet, wild roses, hawthorns.

It's these more open types that are of greatest interest, since dense, impenetrable thickets are really of limited use. Incidentally, many shrublands persist because the shrubs are resistant to grazing animals, being tough, unpalatable and thorny. Shrub-dominated areas have been considered wasteland – unproductive and of limited value – and perhaps this is one reason why they have not been considered to be very attractive. Certainly, the names 'scrub' and 'brush' are not a good starting point! But scrub, for example, is an exciting model for naturalistic planting. It's a bit of a hybrid: a mix of small trees, shrubs and grassland. For example, a vibrant mix of trees and shrubs, most of which are members of the rose family, dominates scrub on limestone or chalk. This includes wild roses themselves of course, but also *Prunus* (cherries), *Sorbus* (rowans and whitebeams), *Crataegus* (hawthorns), *Malus* (crab apples), *Sambucus* (elders), *Ligustrum* (privets), *Viburnum*, *Rubus* (berries) and many others, with vines such as *Clematis*. And all this richness is then mixed with patches of diverse calcareous grassland.

Above: An open woodland edge, with hawthorn, *Crataegus monogyna*, shrubs merging into grassland.

These more open types of shrubland hold the greatest inspiration for me because although the vegetation may be dominated by shrubs they are just part of a mosaic that also includes grasses, herbs, bulbs and small trees – a really attractive proposition. The most effective shrubland landscapes for me are those that create frameworks or spaces in which the more dynamic herbaceous plants can produce sparkling seasonal displays.

Columns and pillars

Shrubs may be used as framing, structural and edge elements (that is, around the edges of spaces), but they also have an important role as internal elements, breaking up space and giving a permanent three-dimensional structure to grasslands or meadows. This idea of punctuation has an important visual quality in breaking the potential monotony of large areas of perennial-dominated vegetation.

THE CEILING

Now we come to the final element in our architectural analogy: what happens overhead. A person experiencing open shrub would have their heads exposed to the sky, and sun and rain would be able to get to ground level. As soon as an overhead layer is included, the experience is completely different. And when I talk about an overhead layer, of course I mean trees.

The experience of woodland or forest largely depends on the dominant tree species, which is partly governed by soil type and climate, but also on the age of the woodland and its successional stage. But broadly we can distinguish between two main types of woodland based on visual character: light woodland and dark woodland.

Light woodlands are composed of relatively short-lived fast-growing trees with open crowns that let a good amount of light through to the ground. These woodlands are often of a pioneer type – that is, the trees are able to colonize bare spaces quickly because they have easily dispersible seeds, and they can establish in conditions of open sun. Birches (*Betula* species) are a perfect example of such a tree. They're often found in large numbers at quite close spacings. *Prunus* (cherries), *Sorbus* (whitebeans and rowans), *Alnus* (alders) and *Fraxinus* (ash) are more examples. Because the canopies of woodlands made up of trees such as these are quite open and there's a lot of dappled shade, the herbaceous layer at the ground can be relatively grassy or rich.

Top: Dense multi-layered woodland, with herbaceous, shrub and tree layers – but there are further layers within each of these layers!

Bottom: A 'light' woodland, such as this birch grove is open with dappled shade.

Dark woodlands are composed of longer-lived and bigger 'forest trees'. Typically they will have more dense and heavy canopies that let much less light through to the ground. The herbaceous layer will mostly be in evidence in the spring, as wildflowers make the most of warmer conditions before the trees come fully into leaf; apart from those there will be evergreens such as ferns that are able to tick along in the shade. Typically dark woodland species are *Quercus* (oak), *Tilia* (limes or lindens) and *Fagus* (beech).

The seeds and young saplings of trees such as these do not germinate and establish well in full sun; they need an overhead canopy to ensure success. They will therefore thrive under the canopy of the pioneer woodlands and gradually grow up through the canopy of the shorter-lived trees, eventually forming the mature woodland. These two simple woodland types are therefore part of a dynamic successional process.

Forest and woodland is only one model of naturalistic tree-based vegetation. As we've seen, different tree and forest types can have a completely different atmosphere according to the tree species. Another determining factor is the density of the trees.

Where trees become more scattered and are set within a predominantly open landscape, then we find savannah vegetation. Savannah occurs where trees don't form a complete canopy, allowing light to ground level, and this promotes a predominantly herbaceous grassland layer beneath, although shrubs are also common. According to the degree of dispersion, trees may be widely scattered or occur at quite high density, and will usually be arranged according to the centre of gravity aggregation pattern, but regardless, there is still enough sense of numbers to create the sense of enclosure and a ceiling in the landscape.

We can think of dispersion in a different way: how closed or open is a landscape? Dense, dark woodlands feel very different to more open and dispersed canopies. We can play with this idea on a larger scale, by imagining journeys through closed, open, half-closed areas, and the different experiences this gives to us. This idea played a big part in the design of the Amstelveen Heem Parks.

Top: A 'dark' woodland composed mainly of forest canopy species, such as these oaks has a strong and powerful character, even in winter when the leaves are off the trees.

Bottom left: The 'stratification' or layering is very clear to see in this wet woodland.

Bottom right: Open woodland, with scattered trees, lets plenty of light through to ground level, while still having a strongly enclosing character.

PLANTING DESIGN PRINCIPLES DERIVED FROM NATURE

I have a set of principles that define my planting design thinking, and they are all derived from what I see in the natural world. It's my 'world view', if you like, and it relates directly to the building blocks idea that we've already discussed and how to use not just herbaceous or perennial plants, but trees and shrubs too. I shall describe and illustrate each one with examples (which are not in any order of priority). To do this, we're going to use a main 'reference landscape'. Using one reference landscape allows us to see how all of these principles play out in a single area. However, I will use many other examples as well, to emphasise the points I am making. But before we go on, I have to highlight again one important point. I'm not in any way saying that these are typical examples of natural landscapes, or that you will find this sort of thing everywhere. However, these are the sort of natural landscapes that inspire me, and that inform what I do, and that help me develop the idea of 'enhanced nature' for planting design.

I'm going to take us to Shangri-La – originally a fictional land, an earthly paradise, featured in the 1933 novel *The Lost Horizon*, by James Hilton. The modern Shangri-La City in the Chinese province of Yunnan is a much more recent phenomenon, named thus in 2001 to attract tourists, but much of what I saw in the surrounding landscape when I visited extensively in 2015 more than lived up to Hilton's fantasy. I had gone to search out examples of beautiful remnant hay meadows that I had been told would leave me speechless. As has happened in much of the West, the former species-rich traditionally managed agricultural landscape has largely disappeared through ploughing, draining and reseeding, but fragments of the original remain, often in remote areas. In fact, some of these areas were so remote that we could only reach them by being punted along upland rivers, until we saw a splash of pink or purple in a field in the distance, indicating a mass of primulas in full flower in a wet meadow. The main example that I'm using here is of just one such area of remnant meadows, scrub and wetlands.

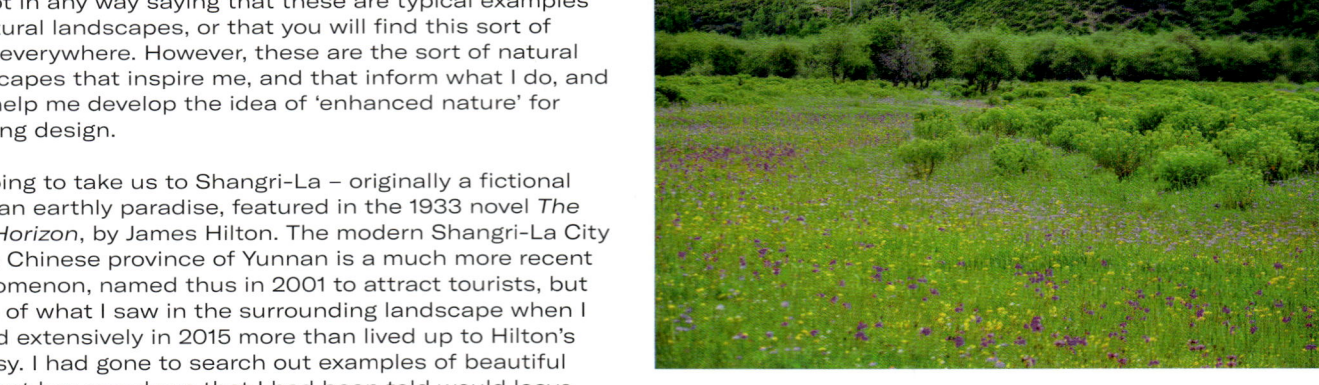

Right: This meadow near Shangri-La, Yunnan is our reference model which will be used to make a series of points, sometimes backed up by examples from elsewhere. There are several different meadow plant communities here with purple *Primula poissonii* a notable species in the foreground and a taller plant community behind with green *Euphorbia jolkinii*.

The power of three

There's a tendency to think that ecologically inspired and naturalistic plantings need to be diverse, with large numbers of different plants in them. Look at any plant or seed list of a naturalistic planting scheme, and generally this list will be long. Diversity is of course really important: greater plant diversity gives rise to greater animal diversity, and more diverse systems are generally more resistant to external stresses and disturbances such as drought or freezing, and more able to bounce back because of the greater numbers of potential survivors. But this push for diversity can be a double-edged sword, encouraging the throwing in of as many different plants as possible, resulting in a patchy, confusing hotch-potch.

In my experience, the most visually satisfying and beautiful 'natural' flowering landscapes are relatively simple in the way they look, and these are the ones that I use as my models. For me, the very best only have one, two, or three visually attractive plants that comprise the main aesthetic experience *at any one time*, and they do this across the entire area of the vegetation. It's my P3 rule – up to three different plants contribute to the visual display at any one time in the most effective and beautiful natural reference points.

Above: In the Shangri-La reference meadow, only two species are making up the visual display at the time the photo was taken, although these are very species-diverse meadows.

Eruptions of colour

The above is not an argument for reducing diversity. All of the examples I give are highly diverse, containing perhaps 20–30 different plant species. It's simply that only three or fewer are performing at their peak at any one time. Go back to these same examples a few weeks earlier or later, and it's likely that one, two or three other plant species are looking fantastic. In these inspirational examples, there's a continuous succession of flowering over months. Imagine a fixed-point time-lapse movie taken of such an area – it would be an ever-changing extravaganza of visual delight, with waves of colour moving back and forth. This idea of 'waves of colour' washing over a planting, garden or landscape is central to my thinking – but only composed of up to three different plants at any one time – the P^3 rule! It's a very dynamic way of thinking.

Another way to visualize this is as eruptions of colour or form happening continuously through a planting – can there be a more dynamic metaphor! Think about a bubbling lava flow, or even slowly boiling water in a pan – eruptions splutter up across the entire surface over a period of time, sometimes in the same place, more often in different places, so that it's a continuous sequence of highlights and subsidence across the entire area.

Above: In our reference meadow, only a small proportion of the total number of species are flowering at any one time. Go back a few weeks later, and a different set of plants will be in flower, part of a continual succession of 'eruptions of colour'.

Opposite top: Repeating drifts of pink *Persicaria bistorta*, scattered *Iris bulleyana* and clumps of *Euphorbia jolkinii* create eruptions of colour across the field in the Shangri-La reference model.

Opposite bottom: Now the three plants in flower in the reference meadow are yellow *Primula sikkimensis*, blue *Cynoglossum amabile* and purple *Pedicularis siphonantha*.

Phenology

An important principle in understanding how this works is the scientific concept of phenology, which describes the seasonal changes in a plant's life-cycle over a year, in particular the patterns of growth, flowering and what happens after flowering. For example, when does it come into growth in the spring, when is its fastest rate of growth, when does it flower and for how long, and does it collapse or remain structurally sound after flowering? The interplay of different plants with different phenologies in a plant community is what gives rise to the visual display over time, and it's something that we can work with very effectively in putting together designed plantings. In other words, we need to aim for a 'phenological mix'.

This scrub plant community in the Shangri-La reference model perfectly illustrates the idea of phenology and length of visual interest. In the top picture *Euphorbia jolkinii* is the species in full flower and it's growing within a shrubby matrix with the large-leaved forb *Ligularia macrophylla*. The foliage of the euphorbia turns bright orange, crimson and scarlet in the autumn, creating spectacular scenes. The ligularia foliage is dramatic in itself, pushing through gaps in the shrubby vegetation. Later, (see picture right) the ligularia flowers with tall yellow daisies, here among silver-leaved artemisias.

May   June   July   August   September

Height

Flowering Period

- Veronica chamaedrys
- Stachys betonica
- Centaurea nigra
- Leucanthemum vulgare
- Sanguisorba officinalis

Above: This diagram shows the differences in phenology of five species in a damp grassland plant community in the north of England. These records are taken from weekly measurements of the growth of plants in a single 500 x 500mm (20 x 20in) 'quadrant'. *Veronica officinalis* (speedwell) is a low creeping plant that flowers in spring and early summer. *Sanguisorba officinalis* (great burnet) is a taller species that flowers in late summer and early autumn. The changes in relative height over the period, and the main flowering times, demonstrate how the 'phenology' of different plant species can be markedly different. It also demonstrates 'layering' in a plant community. This natural example shows how combinations of plants with the same ecological requirements but different phenologies can be combined to create long-season plantings.

Natural layers

We're used to thinking of woodlands as a series of layers. At its simplest, this consists of the tree canopy forming an overhead layer; a shrub layer of multi-stemmed woody plants and sapling trees that can persist beneath the shade canopy; and the field layer or forest floor, composed of shade-tolerant or adapted herbaceous plants. In reality there may be many more layers in a woodland or forest, or indeed fewer.

What is less obvious is that this same layering also happens in grasslands, meadows and other herbaceous plant communities. But unlike the example of a forest, where this is a permanent situation, in the case of herbaceous communities that die back every year or are managed by mowing, cutting or burning, this layering builds up over the course of a single growing season.

The ecological function of layering in plant communities is to maximize their productivity and exploit every possible resource, and plants are adapted to fit their own particular niche; the layering in a forest or in grassland allows the maximum amount of light to be utilized for photosynthesis in that system, for example. In grassland, early-flowering plants are usually short in stature, start into growth rapidly and then tend to tick over amid the taller-growing, later-flowering plants. The latter may be slower in their initial growth, but they then build up a greater bulk and become taller over the entire growing season. Similarly, in woodland, many of the most dramatic flowering plants of the forest floor will come into growth early and flower before the dense heavy shade of the tree canopy takes full effect.

So, the different layers rise up through the ones beneath, according to the growth form and characteristics of the plants involved. A key term here is succession – one thing follows on from another, and each layer pushes up through the one that is already there. Phenology and layering are therefore completely intertwined.

Top: In the primula meadow of our Shangri-La reference model, the different layers are easy to see, with flowers of white *Caltha palustris* species among the grasses, and *Primula poissonii* and a senecio species forming a higher layer.

Opposite: In this North American prairie, a spring layer of prairie phlox flowers among the foliage of later-flowering plants – note the cut-leaved foliage of *Silphium perfoliatum* and the density of plants that will contribute to taller layers later in the growing season.

Flows and drifts

There is usually an underlying structure and pattern within plant communities and landscapes, even though we might look at an area of meadow and grassland and think it's rather uniform. One of the most common organizing principles is the idea of 'flow'. Flow is about directional movement. It's a fluid, sinuous word, implying linkage and continuity. Fluidity is the point here. The flow of water can be the main determining factor in plant distribution patterns, even in very dry landscapes. Tiny differences in the height of the ground can result in it being slightly drier or wetter, and different plant communities will organize themselves according to this. Over time, water-flows form a meandering pattern of sweeping sinuous curves. This meandering, sinuous form is one that I use frequently.

The idea of directional movement lies at the heart of the drift. We tend to think of drifts as being about single plant species, perhaps arising from the spreading clonal growth of a plant, or because many seedlings have established around an original parent. But drifts are just as likely to be about mixes or combinations of plants, or entire plant communities, all responding to minute or obvious differences in topography, drainage, nutrient availability, and many other factors across a site.

Flows and drifts in a landscape have several aesthetic characteristics. Their directional nature leads the eye into and through the landscape, giving legibility to what might otherwise be a featureless or monotonous mass; and they set up a rhythm of repetition across the area, again giving important structure and organization.

Top: Flowing patterns in our reference Shangri-La meadow.

Left: Rather than being completely randomly or uniformly distributed, plants in meadow-like communities tend to occur in drifts. Often this is only apparent when you step back and take a bigger view, as is seen in our reference Shangri-La meadow.

Fuzzy edges

Although seemingly monotonous and uniform areas of vegetation are often in reality composed of well-defined zones, drifts or flows of different plant combinations or communities, this is usually only apparent at the larger scale. At a smaller scale or individual areas of vegetation, this distinction can be much less obvious. This can cause problems: the scale at which ecologically inspired designers often look for inspiration is within individual plant communities or vegetation types, and they are therefore in danger of missing the bigger picture.

When you get down to the smaller scale you realize that what seem like clear and distinct boundaries at the larger scale are actually indistinct. There's a merging and interaction at the edges. In other words, we are dealing with fuzzy edges. That's because abrupt boundaries and black and white differences are quite rare in plant ecology. Site conditions tend to vary along a gradient of change rather than switching on and off. Individual species bleed in and out of mixes and plant communities. As a result, change occurs along a transition zone rather than abruptly. This leads to many exciting combinations and interactions.

Above: Although drift patterns can be clearly seen at the larger scale in the Shangri-La reference meadow, it becomes apparent that at the smaller scale the interactions between these drifts are complex. There are no distinct boundaries between drifts – the edges are fuzzy.

Above: In our Shangri-La reference meadow, the blue-flowered *Aster tongolensis* takes the role of a 'cross-over' species, being a component of several different mixes and drifts within the meadow as a whole.

Cross-overs

The concept of gradients leads us on to another very important observation. Plant species inhabit their own areas of preference along environmental gradients (for example a gradient of soil wetness or of nutrient availability). Those preferences might be quite precise or they might be very broad. There's a lot of cross-over of species along these gradients, and what we might see as distinct plant communities at any one point are really collections of species that happen to coincide under those conditions.

It follows that some species might occur in several adjacent plant communities or mixtures in any given area, while others might be confined to fewer or only one of them. The more widely occurring or 'cross-over' species are important in giving coherence and unity across what otherwise might be visually or ecologically different plant communities.

Centres of gravity

Now, let's look in more detail at the patterns in which the plants are arranged. I want to introduce a universal pattern that relates to the way that plants grow in the wild. Technically it's called aggregation, but I prefer to think of it as 'centres of gravity'. We'll return to this idea many times throughout this chapter and explore the concept further in the next, but the purpose here is to be able to recognize it.

Imagine what it would look like if a plant were uniformly distributed across an area of space. All the individuals or groups of that plant would occur at roughly the same distance from each other, at roughly the same density. In effect it would be the same as is found in a forest plantation, or in an agricultural crop field – or, for that matter, in a traditional horticultural planting. That doesn't feel very natural, does it? But it is how we tend to think of the way plants might grow in a meadow or other types of grassland, for example, and when you work with seed mixes or random planting mixes then this is the starting point – all the seeds or plants are spread evenly across an entire area.

The reality is that plants tend to organize themselves through various forms of clustering or clumping. The clumping might be very tight or very loose, but it will be there. It's all a matter of the scale at which you observe the vegetation. Even in its tightest form, where a species might form large spreading masses (monocultures, or drifts) these masses will themselves be clustered or clumped at the bigger scale. This patterning is the result of two main factors: a) variation in physical factors across a site (such as moisture availability or nutrient levels) which in turn influence the distribution of plants; and b) the growth patterns and characteristics of the individual species themselves.

The study of how plant species arrange themselves in these sorts of patterns has been a strong element in the technocratic strand of naturalistic planting design discussed earlier in this book. It's known as 'plant sociability', which basically translates into how 'friendly' individuals of a species are with each other! There's a scale of sociability going from dense monocultures where the individuals are very 'friendly' right through to widely scattered and anti-social plants where there is little or no relationship between any individuals. Although it's important to understand the basis of this, the key thing is to be aware of how this works out on the ground in visual terms.

The concept of 'centres of gravity' is a more visual way to describe this. The pattern I come across again and again could best be described as a 'centre with outliers'. Imagine a tray full of small loose metal spheres or ball bearings. Now put a magnet in among them, and depending how close they are to the magnet some of the spheres will be attracted and gather around it and others will move just a small distance. There will be an aggregated centre of spheres with more widely distributed spheres further

Top: *Euphorbia jolkinii* forming an aggregated pattern with outliers along with *Aster tongolensis* and *Cynoglossum amabile* in our Shangri-La reference model.

Middle: *Iris bulleyana* in aggregated clumps in the meadow with *Euphorbia jolkinii*.

Bottom: The same aggregated pattern with outliers is apparent in our Shangri-La reference meadow, for both *Primula poissonii* and the yellow *Pedicularis* species.

away. If it's a strong magnet there will be a dense centre with many spheres, while in the case of a weak magnet there might be hardly any. And then, if you put in several magnets spaced apart, you will get a repetition of that pattern. I don't want to stretch the metaphor any further, but this type of pattern occurs at all scales and in a huge variety of contexts, from the patterns of lichens on a single rock through to the distributions of tree species across entire forests.

The diagram here is modified from a figure in Peter Greig-Smith's book *Quantitative Plant Ecology* (1983) and in that book is captioned 'Patches of higher density imposed on a general distribution of lower density, a type of plant distribution commonly encountered.' Each dot is an individual plant and they are all of the same species. There's no scale because, as I noted above, this could apply to any type of plant anywhere.

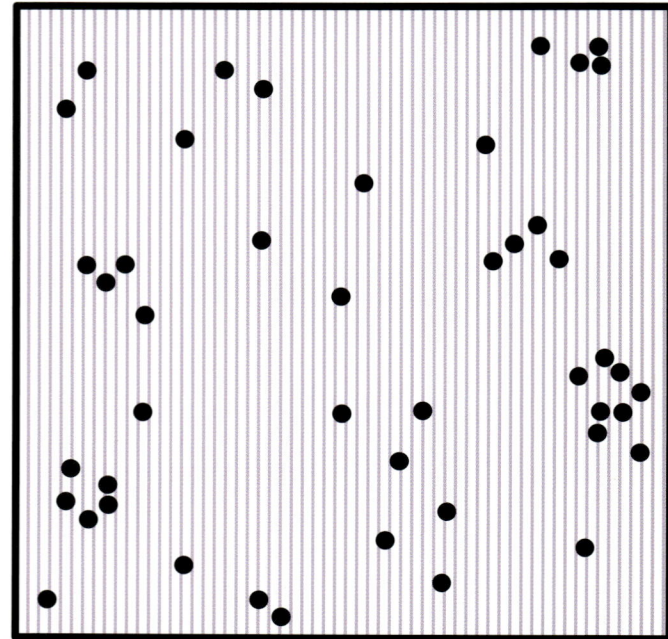

Below: The pattern of these plants (*Stellera chamaejasme* var. *chrysantha*) in a field near our Shangri-La reference meadow, would be very different if they were all uniformly and equally spaced.

Repetition and rhythm

Rhythm implies repetition, but it also suggests a certain order and predictability. Look again at many of the images in this chapter, and you'll see repetition of drifts, of plant forms, of individuals themselves. It's one of the most important factors that turns an attractive landscape into an extraordinary one. That's because it allows us to transform what might otherwise be a chaotic and random amalgam into something that we can make sense of. Repetition and rhythm might be apparent in colours or textures, but one of the most visually striking aspects is form – the shape and three-dimensional structure of plants in the landscape. Nowhere is this more clearly demonstrated than with the concept of emergents. These are plants that protrude above the general mass, and typically the most prominent ones are upright in form. A single emergent plant in a sea of lower-growing plants isn't going to make much of an impact, but repetition across an area starts to create a real sense of drama. Uniform repetition is one thing, but when there is a sense of rhythm and something a bit more complex than everything looking the same, this becomes very special.

Top: Repetition of clumps and drifts, including yellow *Potentilla chinensis*, across the whole area, sets up a rhythm of colours and textures.

Above: The repetition of scattered individuals of smoke bush, *Cotinus coggygria*, in open dry scrub, leads the eye on through the landscape.

Complex edges

Edges are an important concept in ecology, because it's here that a lot of the action takes place. The transitions between two or more different vegetation types, such as forest and grassland, are technically termed 'ecotones'. Where such transitions occur the characteristics of both types combine, and the visual complexity and the wildlife and biodiversity value can be maximized. This is a particularly useful natural model for small spaces, where working with edges and ecotones provides a huge scope.

At this point, we can't avoid discussing an observation from the natural world that is very controversial among garden designers and landscape architects: there are few straight lines in nature. Edges in nature are complex and rough. It's easy to see why this is: maintaining straight-line edges requires a lot of energy and input. We only find these in managed or designed landscapes, preserved by ongoing maintenance – horticultural or agricultural.

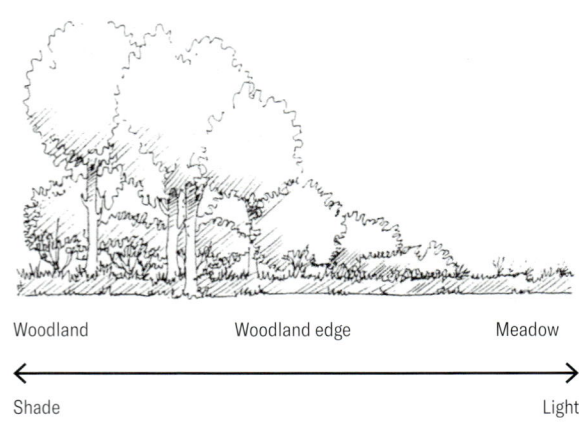

Woodland   Woodland edge   Meadow

←——————————————————————→

Shade   Light

Complex edges are an extension of the concept of fuzzy edges. This complexity occurs in both horizontal and vertical space. We can explore this best by looking at woodland or forest edges, and in so doing, considering trees as well as shrubs. Woodland edges can combine elements of grasslands, shrublands and the woodland itself, all in a relatively narrow ecotone area. Shrubs and trees will spill out into the grassland, sometimes for some distance, and the grassland will encroach into the edge of the woodland or beyond.

Because there's an abundance of light on the edges compared to a forest interior, this is the place where there will be the highest concentration of flowering and fruiting shrubs and trees, and also vines and climbers. These of course will be affected by aspect. In the Northern Hemisphere, south-facing edges will be the sunniest, warmest and most sheltered. It's here that the greatest numbers of flowers and fruits will be found, and also the largest numbers of invertebrates and birds. Coincidentally, these will also be the most attractive for people too. Conversely, cool, largely shaded north-facing edges will be less rich in flowers, fruit and wildlife. The opposite is clearly the case in the Southern Hemisphere.

Above and left: Straight-line edges and simple, clear-cut boundaries between one vegetation type and another are rare in natural systems. In this dry meadow in Austria, where the yellow bracts of *Euphorbia cyparissias* are prominent, there is a boundary of woodland beyond but shrubs are encroaching into the grassland to a considerable distance. If you were to draw a plan of this vegetation, as seen from above, a very complex pattern of gradation from open grassland to denser shrub and tree mass would be evident. The scattered shrubs in the foreground act as 'pillars' (see page 79) giving a valuable three-dimensional structure to the otherwise uniform grassland.

The immersive experience

This is one of the special qualities of naturalistic landscapes, offering something very different to the usual experience of gardens. Being immersed in nature is a total, multi-sensory experience – not just visual appreciation, but also sound, touch, smell, movement, intimate experience of other life as well as your own. At some point in your life you may have followed a track that has taken you directly into just this kind of all-enveloping vegetation. It's impossible not to actively engage with nature in such a form; compare that to most garden or designed landscape experiences, which are very passive affairs. Plantings are often in beds, and you look at them from a lawn or area of hard surface. Crucially, you are standing apart from the planting, uninvolved. The active, involved, multi-sensory experience one gains from being immersed in an inspirational natural landscape is one of the most important principles in this book and it is a vital constituent of my design work.

Top: The merging of the meadow into the scrubby edge is an example of an ecotone.

Above: The experience of walking along this path through a prairie in spring is immersive, and very different from the way we normally interact with vegetation in designed landscapes.

Reading Nature 97

Cultural context

I've already noted that when I refer to 'natural' landscapes, what I really mean is 'semi-natural', because virtually all landscapes, vegetations and plant communities have been modified by human beings. However, our influence goes beyond merely adapting plant communities. There's a cultural layer to the landscape too that generates further 'plant signatures'. These recognizable linkages between certain plants or assemblages of plants and cultural artefacts in the landscape can be useful as additional elements to provide a starting point, or 'design generator', for a composition. The important point here is that, where appropriate, t can be used to introduce a distinctive element to a planting that gives it a reference to the locality – a sense of place.

Opposite top: Isolated groups of thorny or tough shrubs or small trees n areas, such as this steppe with pink *Dictamnus albus*, are characteristic of landscapes that have a long history of human use. The multi-stem tree here in a large expanse of grassland demonstrates the essential need for structure and 'punctuation' in what would otherwise be a relatively two-dimensional and rather monotonous view.

Opposite bottom: The multitude of rounded forms of oaks and willows in this landscape in the Lake District, Cumbria is regularly grazed (the grazing line at sheep head height can be seen on the trees) and is a form of traditional 'wood pasture'. The upright forms of the rushes and ferns in the foreground are unpalatable to grazers, and so survive. It's a highly cultural landscape, that also in terms of its spatial and structural qualities, provides much design inspiration.

Below: An ancient apple orchard with wildflowers beneath has a romantic, natural appeal and yet represents a landscape that is totally modified by humans.

PLANT STRATEGY THEORY

In the concluding part of this chapter, we're going to take a step back and look at the processes driving the patterns that we've already noted.

Plant strategy theory – the key to understanding how plant communities work – was developed by Professor Philip Grime and colleagues at the University of Sheffield and is one of the foremost global theories in plant ecology. Phil Grime was my PhD supervisor, so I know this theory very well: my PhD was all about it. Although many other authors have attempted to apply the theory to horticulture and planting design, they have all used the original ecological terminology, and this doesn't translate so easily into an applied field.

Stress and disturbance

The basis of plant strategy theory is the idea that there are two basic forces that act upon plants in any given area and limit their optimal performance. The first of these, known as stress, is anything that reduces the growth rate of a plant and the amount of total 'biomass' that the plant can produce. So, stress factors might include low nutrient levels, too little or too much water, and extreme cold or heat. For example, very dry climates or very infertile soil will be stressful to plants that are not specially adapted to these conditions. Give them a bit more water or some fertilizer and they will gallop away. In other words, the stressful conditions are holding the plants back from reaching their full growth potential through reducing the amount of biomass that they are able to produce.

In low-stress environments, there's nothing to hold back plants from reaching their highest growth potential. Such sites are more fertile, have adequate supplies of water, mild temperatures and so on. We can therefore characterize low-stress environments as highly productive, and conversely, high-stress environments as very unproductive.

The other main force is known as disturbance – anything that causes damage to existing plant growth. This could be grazing, trampling, burning, cultivation or severe drought. Plants may be growing in a very low-stress environment, and therefore potentially able to reach their full growth potential, but if some external agent is regularly damaging them, this potential will not be reached. Instead of reducing growth rates, disturbance destroys plant material that has already been made.

Very disturbed environments are very unstable, suffering regular disruptions such as severe droughts, regular ploughing, flooding, and so on. Conversely, environments with minimal disturbance are very stable.

Productivity and stability

The underlying principle behind plant strategy theory is that every place in the world can be defined by its relative degrees of productivity and stability. Plants have adapted themselves over evolutionary time to be able to survive in these different types of environment. And here's the thing: plants tend to have the same types of adaptations to stress and disturbance, regardless of where in the world they are and what type of stress and disturbance affects them. As a result we can classify plants, plant communities and vegetation types according to their suitability to these different combinations of productivity and stability. In the graph opposite, stress and disturbance are measured on an index of 0 to 10, and they are expressed in terms of productivity and stability. This index is purely relative.

In the lower left corner, we have the combination of very productive and very stable conditions. For a traditional garden or landscape setting, this is the thing that everybody strives for – perfect conditions for plant growth in the form of abundant nutrients and water, benign temperatures and complete lack of any damage. However, in the wild, the story is very different. In environments where there is nothing to put a brake on plant growth, plants that can exploit these conditions to the utmost are favoured: rapid growers and spreaders that occupy as much space above and below ground as they can so that they can grab the maximum water, nutrients and light. Such plants are aggressive and very competitive, eliminating weaker or more delicate plants that are unable to keep up. Let's describe this type of plant as 'dominators' (called competitors in the original theory) because they tend to take over space for themselves, resulting in very low-diversity vegetation, often with very coarse plants.

Right: A graph to show the effects of stability (degree of stress or disturbance) on the productivity of three different types of plant.

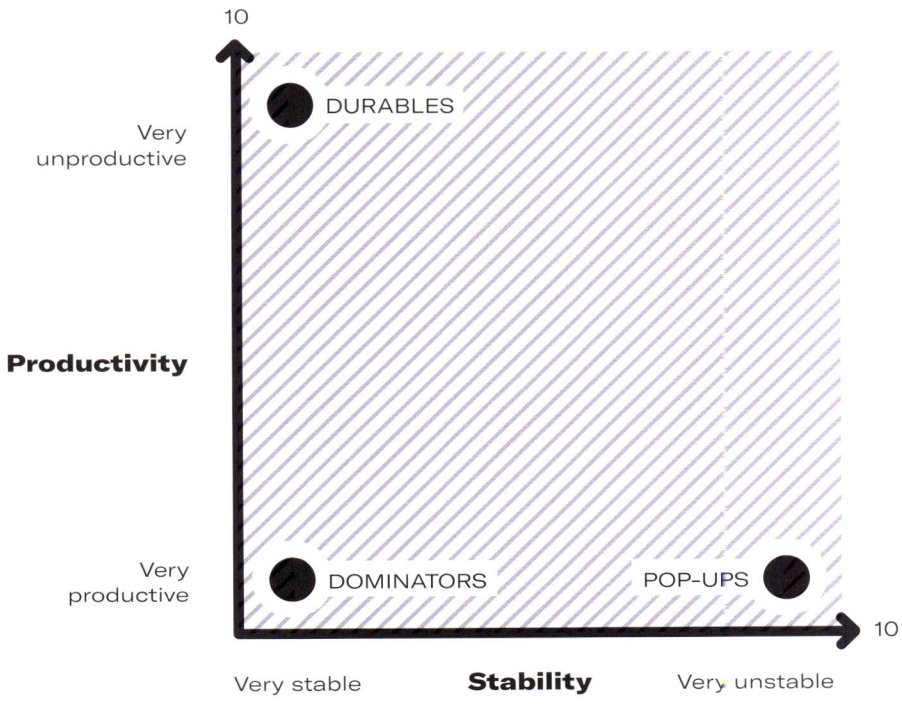

Above: This abandoned, unmanaged and very fertile former urban allotment site has become over-run by a classic 'dominator' plant, *Chamerion angustifolium*, rosebay willowherb. Very few, if any, other species are likely to co-exist amongst the vigorous clonal 'stands' of this highly competitive plant.

Conversely, in very disturbed, unstable places, there just isn't the chance for these dominators to get a toe-hold – they are constantly being damaged or destroyed. Take a regularly cultivated field, for example, where all the existing vegetation is destroyed at least once a year. A new crop might be sown or planted, but if that field were to be left alone after cultivation, it would soon fill up with plants that are usually called weeds. We'll call them 'pop-ups' (named as ruderals in the original theory), and they fit in the bottom right corner of the graph, where conditions are still fertile and productive, but very unstable. In order to survive the cycles of disturbance, plants are short-lived – annuals, biennials, short-lived perennials. They are good at dispersing by seed or other means so that they are able to escape the disturbed areas and find new places to colonize. Some plant communities that fall into this category are among the most spectacular on the planet: the desert blooms of the south-western United States and South Africa are two well-known examples, where whole landscapes light up with annuals that respond to spring rains and germinate, flower and drop their seed before the onset of the ferocious summer drought.

Top: Annuals are classic 'pop-up' or disturbance-tolerant plants that complete their life cycle in a single growing season between disturbance events. This seeded annual flower field at Trentham Gardens, Staffordshire features orange California poppy, *Eschscholtzia californica*, and blue tansy, *Phaecelia tanacetifolia*.

Above left: A whole range of pioneer 'pop-up' plants have colonized this abandoned, post-industrial site in Sheffield. Both the North American Michaelmas daisy, *Aster novi-belgii*, and the silver birch, *Betula pendula*, have been able to reach this site because they produce copious wind-blown seed and are able to establish on open sites with skeletal soils.

Above right: Another Sheffield post-industrial site, covered with building demolition material, has been colonized by biennial and short-lived perennial 'pop-up' plants, including purple toadflax, *Linaria purpurea*, and weld, *Resedea luteola*.

In places that are relatively stable but very unproductive, conditions are tough, with extreme temperatures, low nutrient and water availability, and thin, rocky soils. Plants that survive under these extreme conditions have many adaptations that enable them to do this: slow growth, low-growing rounded forms, tough leaves and stems. Let's call them 'durables' (stress-tolerators in the original theory). Plant communities that exhibit durable characteristics include those from dry and arid environments, where plants have adaptations to conserve water, such as grey, silver or blue-green foliage (caused by minute hairs or thick waxy cuticles), succulent characteristics, or low cushion-like growth. Alpine plants are another example: their low, creeping, ground-hugging forms or tight rosettes combat the high exposure and low temperatures of high altitude environments.

There are many intermediate categories between these three extremes, but there's no category for a combination of a highly unproductive and highly unstable environment – that describes a scenario where it's impossible for plant life to survive.

Above: Plants in the acid heathland (above), and the dry scrub (below) have similar adaptations to high stress, even though the climate is very different.

Diversity

This brief review of plant strategy theory leads us to an important conclusion. The growing conditions that we aim to promote for plants in traditional garden and landscape settings are the very ones that are not advantageous to the development of diverse and attractive natural vegetations in the wild. Indeed, they foster aggressive, vigorous dominator plants in the landscape. Conversely, settings that are extreme in their degree of stress and disturbance are very hostile to plant growth. The environmental conditions that promote the kind of diverse and beautiful plant communities that have been featured in this chapter are those in which there are moderate levels of stress and/or disturbance. This is an important point to bear in mind when we move on to consider the conditions that we ourselves will need to create in order to produce our own diverse and beautiful naturalistic plantings, both in terms of establishment conditions and on-going maintenance. And that leads us on to the next chapter: how to apply the principles that I've outlined here to our own ways of working with plants.

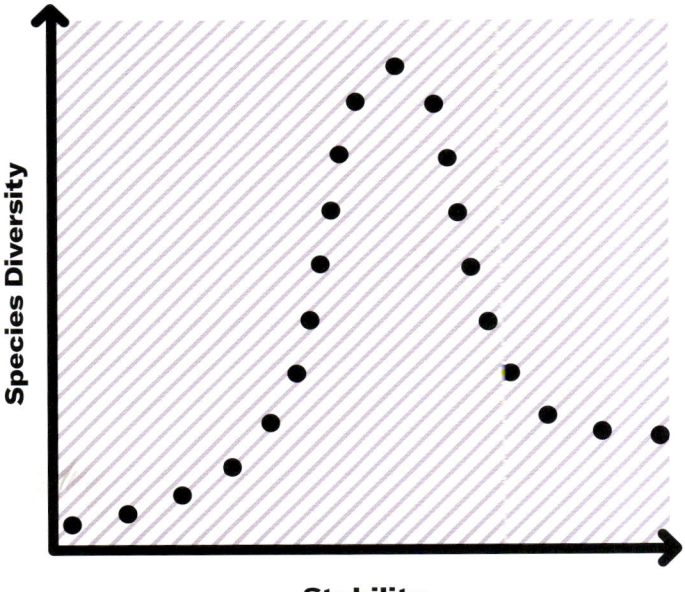

Very unstable: high levels of stress and/or disturbance

Very stable: minimal levels of stress and/or disturbance

Above: The humpback model in ecology explains the relationship between plant diversity and dominant site conditions. The graph shows how plant diversity changes with site stability. In both very unstable sites (highly disturbed and or very infertile) and very stable (very fertile and/or undisturbed) diversity is low because conditions in the former are very hostile to plant growth, and in the latter are favourable to aggressive 'dominator' plants that eliminate all less competitive plants. The big lesson from this model is that the highest plant diversity is promoted by moderate levels of stress and disturbance in the system.

Reading Nature

PLANTING DESIGN TOOLKIT

In the last chapter I described some general patterns in wild or semi-natural vegetation that form the basis for my own planting design approach. In this chapter I'll be discussing how to apply these concepts. My aim is to present a straightforward set of methods that can be used to develop the sort of exuberant plantings that this book is about rather than bogging you down with a huge amount of technical detail. There isn't a plant directory, or recommended lists of plants, because this is more about a set of ideas, a philosophy and a series of underlying considerations and steps. It's a starting point or launch pad for developing all sorts of exciting new plant combinations as well as tried-and-tested ones, and for adapting the ideas into different climate zones. So, let's move on to looking at how I apply my own 'natural inspiration' into the way that I work with plants.

MAKING SPACES

I want to see and encourage this type of planting to be used on a widespread basis: for it to become mainstream rather than a niche interest. That's not going to happen if the technicalities are so daunting that most people are put off even trying to have a go. That's not to say that it's altogether easy, since there are important ideas that need to be borne in mind – but I hope to demystify it, and to sieve out all but the most essential nuggets of information. As discussed earlier, naturalistic planting design has split into several quite different strands, and this is a good point at which to bring some of these together and to work with the best ideas from all of them.

The main content of this chapter is concerned with the detail of organizing individual areas of planting, but first we need to look at the bigger picture and consider how naturalistic principles might be used to structure designed landscapes in the first place.

I have discussed the idea of using planting to *make* spaces rather than *fill* spaces. So, let's think about applying the principles covered last chapter to the structuring of landscape and garden spaces. I won't go into details about how to design a space: there are many excellent books that explore this in depth. I'm assuming that, regardless of the size of the area that you are dealing with, you've been through some of the basics of site evaluation and know in general terms about your soil type, aspect and microclimate, and the various functions of your space.

It's important to become familiar with local and regional vegetation types and plant communities, getting to know the typical patterns, the key species that define that visual character and cultural overlays. This is not necessarily so that you can copy them; it's more about getting a feel for the character and ecology of the area, so that what you are doing 'fits'.

When it comes down to making spaces, I can't put it any better than Darrel Morrison who I came across during my time with the Garden Club of America in the late 1980s. Darrel was the senior figure in tuned-to-nature planting design in the US, and I immediately found a resonance in his methods with much of what I had been feeling but had been unable to fully express. I was lucky enough to persuade him to write a chapter in *The Dynamic Landscape* (Taylor & Francis, 2007), a book on naturalistic planting design that I co-edited with James Hitchmough. The following sequence of steps is based on Darrel's recommendations from that chapter:

1 Site analysis
As well as broad-scale observations of soils, geology, climate and ecological context, smaller-scale, micro-environmental observations can be of special importance. These might include areas with different shade intensity and duration, poorly drained areas that will be wet for part of the year or very hot dry areas. All of these are influenced by buildings – paved surfaces and south- and west-facing walls, for example, will radiate and reflect heat.

2 User analysis
This is where you identify the main needs of people who will use the space, and their functional requirements. It will examine the main access and circulation routes where paths need to go, and will indicate where specific uses and features are best placed for the convenience of users.

3 Mass-space plan
This concept sits at the core of setting out a naturalistic garden or landscape. The importance of such a plan can't be overstated – it enables the creation of a flowing, cohesive plan. As Darrel says:

'The site analysis will have identified the "given" masses (e.g., buildings and existing vegetation masses), as well as open spaces (e.g., paved surfaces, rock outcroppings, open water, zones of low vegetation). The user analysis will have identified currently open areas where vegetation masses are needed for enclosure, screening, or spatial formation. It will also suggest the need for open spaces to accommodate specific activities. From these two sources, a mass/space plan can be developed.'

4 Assign building blocks
The masses in the mass-space plan can then be translated into the 'walls and ceilings' of the scheme, identifying appropriate structural 'building blocks'. The spaces can be translated into appropriate 'floor plan' building blocks: meadows and wetlands, for example, and lawns or paved surfaces.

5 Choose the plants
At this stage it is appropriate to choose the plant communities and planting in detail to fit the various chosen building blocks.

Opposite: In planting design terms, mass can be simply defined as vegetation that contains or shapes a space, or which impedes or prevents movement, or which blocks sight-lines. And space can be defined as vegetation that fills space, or enables views across it, or which enables easy movement through it. Here, a flowing sequence of open spaces is created by vegetation structures or *mass* at different levels. The lawn is contained by sweeps of taller grass-like sedges. At a higher level, the entire space is defined by the surrounding trees.

Above: Another multi-layered example of mass and space. The open glade is surrounded by oak woodland, and is filled by mixed perennials, ferns and grasses. However, this is further defined by the wide path that weaves around the edge of this ground layer planting.

Previous page: A drift of *Eupatorium hyssopifolium* (hyssopleaf thoroughwort), and the scattered spikes and globular seedheads of *Eryngium yuccifolium* (rattlesnake master) rise up through a matrix layer of the grass *Sporobolus heterolepis* (prairie dropseed), with occasional multi-stem *Betula nigra* (river birch) in a Pennsylvania garden, USA.

Top: These wide open flowing spaces in Jac P Thijssepark, Amstelveen were created by planting multi-layered woodland to frame and shape the open spaces.

Above left: Small interventions can create spatial separation: here a loose line of coppiced willows diverts a path away from the edge of the lake in Reykjavik's central park.

Above right: This space is structured with vegetation in many different ways. The surrounding trees create the atmosphere of an informal glade, and this is further reinforced by loose informal shrubs on the boundary. However, there is a more formal encircling element of a low hedge that bounds the meadowy grassland of the 'floor-plan'. And then within the larger glade is a more private space with a seat, enclosed with a taller hedge.

BUILDING BLOCKS

Once the spatial structure and sequence have been worked out, plant community types can be allocated to build up that structure.

'Architectural' type	Character reference communities	Detail
Floor	Grasslands Wetlands Woodland floor	Meadow Prairie Steppe Flowering lawn Urban recombinant
Walls	Shrublands Woodland edge Pillars and columns	Scrub Coppice
Ceiling		Dark woodland Light woodland Pioneer woodland Savannah Wood pasture Orchard

And then there are many more levels of detail: different types of meadow or light woodland, for example. You can now start to put together combinations of these building blocks to 'construct' your landscape. These combinations are numerous. For example: 'Flowering lawn + meadow + orchard + coppice' begins to describe a very attractive build-up for a semi-open garden with great flowering and structural interest.

At this point we can move on to consider the detail of what happens within these building blocks. The main focus for the rest of this chapter will be on the 'floor level' plantings, since this layer runs as a constant through both of the other types and is where we can really get to grips with the idea of creating the full immersive experience. We're going to consider a general methodology for working with plants that will help you to create the enhanced naturalistic character that this book is all about.

Sheffield General Cemetery: view along the main path with fingers of box (*Buxus sempervirens*) to the right, and a coppice bed to the left. Design: Nigel Dunnett

Planting Design Toolkit

Top left: The coppice bed in spring, with multi-stemmed amelanchier in flower.

Top right: Forsythia used as a woodland edge plant to create a 'ribbon of gold' along the margin of the meadow in early spring.

Middle left: In summer, the forsythia becomes a simple green backdrop to the meadow glade.

Middle right: A white-flowered form of flowering raspberry, *Rubus odoratus* along the woodland edge, with teasels (*Dipsacus fullonum*) in the grassland.

Bottom left: Fingers of box create bays for herbaceous planting.

Bottom right: Perennial planting in early summer, with *Persicaria bistorta*, *Geranium macrorrhizum* and *Geranium sylvaticum* 'Alba' with the coppice bed opposite underplanted with perennials and ferns.

LINE

Before getting to the detail, the first thing I often do is set out a line through the planting area. This line is usually a variation of Hogarth's classic 'line of beauty': a sinuous S-shaped curve. It's a meandering, river-like flow, exactly like the examples shown in the previous chapter. This is an organizing principle, which is also about legibility. It draws the eye through and into the planting area and, even in a very complex scheme, allows the viewer to comprehend the structure in a single glance. This idea works at all scales, enabling a flowing sequence of spaces to be established as the basis for a whole garden or landscape. The line can be used to visually connect nearby or adjacent areas of planting, and within an individual area of planting it provides a starting point for everything else.

It's important to link the direction of flow to align with the main viewing points for the planting. Rarely will this be directly from the front unless there is good depth to the planting area. More usually it will be towards either end to generate the longest possible trajectory for the starting line.

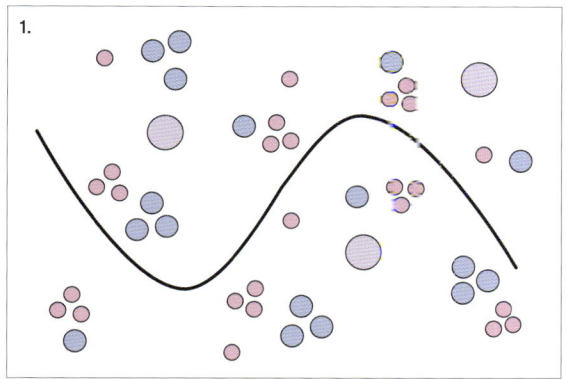

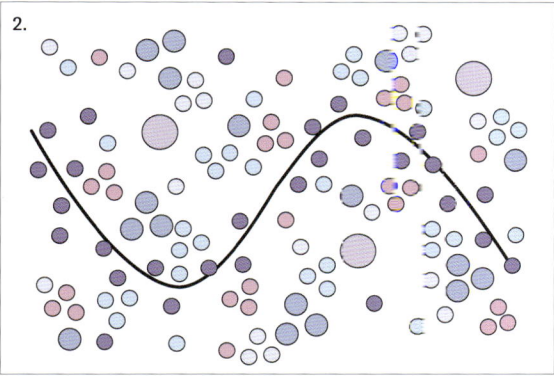

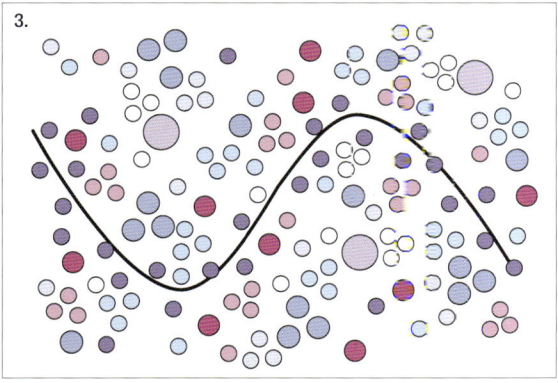

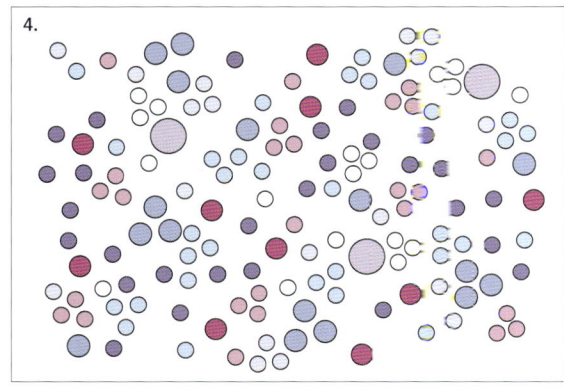

Above: *Campanula lactiflora* 'Loddon Anna' in full flower in the featured planting, with a flowing space between the clumps occupied by the grass, *Calamagrostis brachytricha*.

Right: The diagrams show the build-up of a planting using methods described in full later in this chapter. Each different coloured circle represents a different plant species. In diagram 1, the line guides the placement of the main structural plants. The deep purple circles represent a multi-stem shrub, and these are located first (as a main 'anchor' plant). The light blue circles are significant structural perennials and are located next in loose association with the original anchor plant, and groups of further perennials (pink circles) are then placed in association with them. The arrangement of each of these species follows the aggregated pattern that we discussed in the previous chapter. Diagrams 2 and 3 show the gradual infilling, with further species in aggregated 'Centre of Gravity' clumps. In diagram 4, the original guiding line has been removed. What at first glance might seem a random mix actually has a strong organizational basis.

Planting Design Toolkit

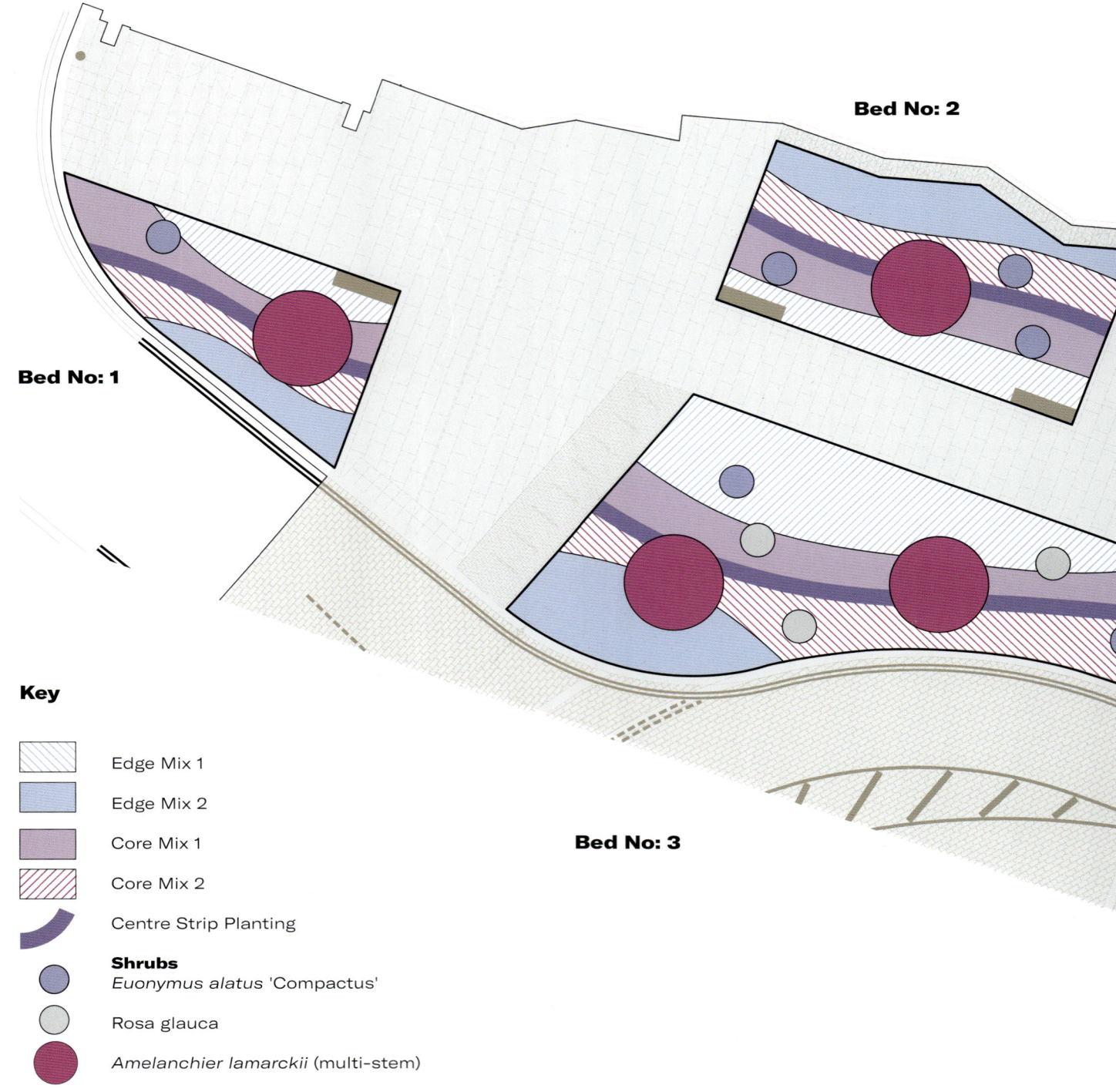

Key

(hatched light)	Edge Mix 1
(light blue)	Edge Mix 2
(mauve)	Core Mix 1
(red hatched)	Core Mix 2
(purple strip)	Centre Strip Planting

Shrubs

- (blue circle) *Euonymus alatus* 'Compactus'
- (grey circle) *Rosa glauca*
- (red circle) *Amelanchier lamarckii* (multi-stem)

This plan shows part of a much larger planting scheme concept for a development at Kings Cross, London. The site consists of a long series of planting areas along a busy pedestrian streetscape. To create coherence and linkage between these separate beds, a line was drawn through all of them to create a visual linkage, and in turn this was translated into a central strip of architectural or structural plants. Four different perennial and grass mixes were located as flowing drifts that followed the original line. A further layer of multi-stem small trees and shrubs were spot located in a more random pattern, but again in a way that was guided by the original line.

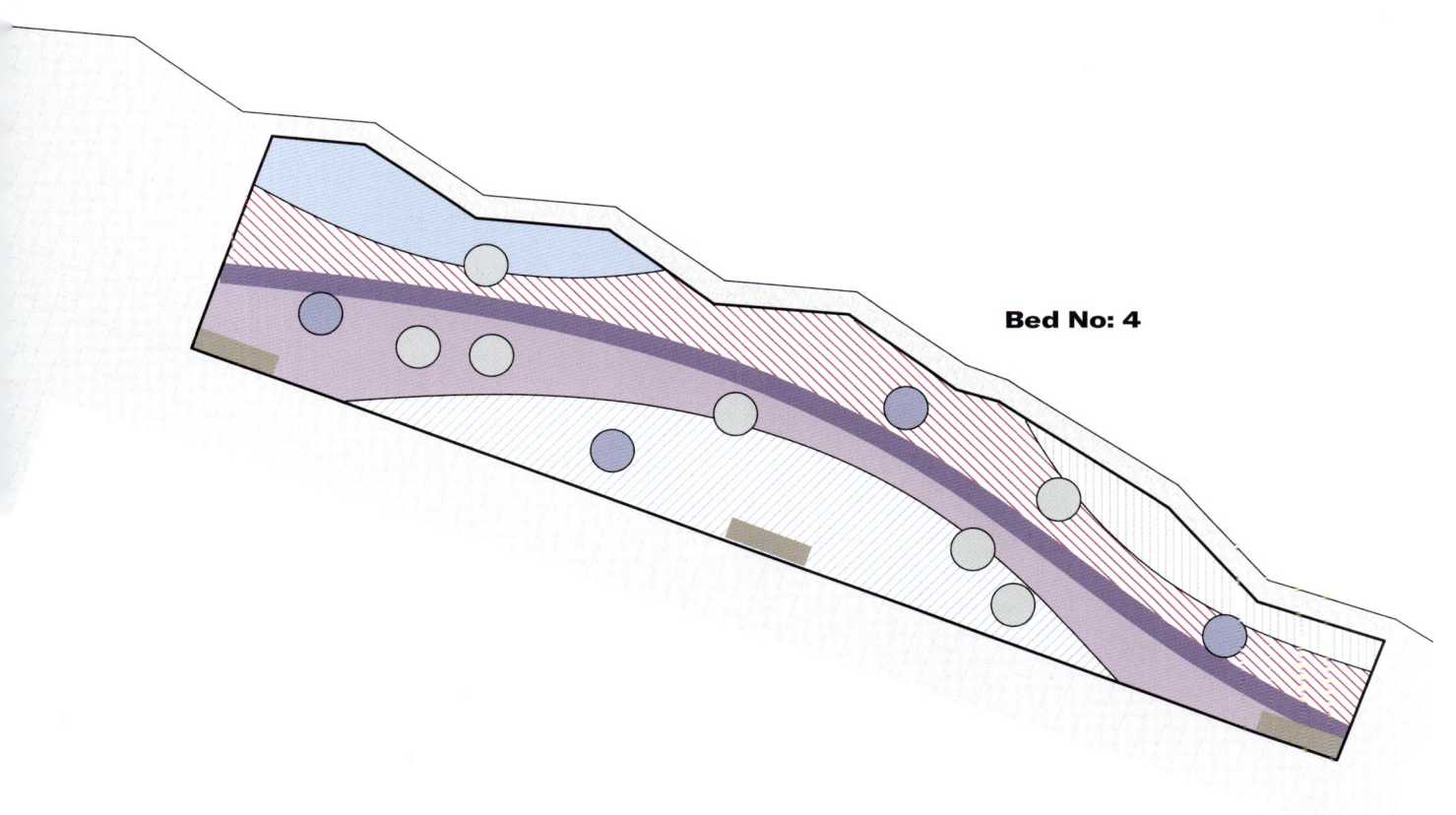

Bed No: 4

Planting Design Toolkit

CASE STUDY: TRENTHAM WOODLAND GARDEN

Design: Nigel Dunnett
Implementation: Spring 2016

The new woodland garden at Trentham Gardesn runs along one side of the Capability Brown lake. Following decades of neglect, the ancient oak woodland was cleared in 2015 of dense *Rhododendron ponticum* undergrowth and a weedy invasion of sycamore (*Acer pseudoplatanus*), resulting in a clean woodland floor and long sight lines beneath the elevated tree canopy.

I wanted to reinvent the idea of the woodland garden and move away from the usual patchy collections of trees and shrubs. Instead, I planned to celebrate the glory of the flowering woodland herbaceous ground layer and to re-create the emotional uplift of woodlands in the wild, full of flowers. As well as the plants of the British woodlands in spring, I also wanted to capture the spectacle of eastern North American forests, with their sheets of *Trillium*, *Tiarella* and *Phlox*. I was heavily influenced by my experiences with the Heem Parks of Amstelveen in my idea of creating a strongly pictorial effect.

But how to go about this? To make the most of the long views, I worked with the idea of long drifts of different perennial, grass and fern mixes, with some cross-over species and mingled edges, using many of the principles outlined in the previous chapter. I set up several curving lines across the site to define the loose boundaries of the mixes. These lines can be extended indefinitely in the future to expand the plantings. I defined the lines with loose strips of ferns, sedges and grasses, which slightly extended into the adjacent mixes and also incorporated some of the plants in those mixes.

Below: The concept for the woodland garden at Trentham Gardens organized around a series of defining lines. First (diagram 1) three lines were drawn along the length of the site, which led to the development of four different flowing drifts of colour-themed perennial mixes. Secondly, to provide contrast, a meandering line was drawn over the top (diagram 2), which resulted in a series of insertions into these drifts. The resulting pattern was then translated into a design that consisted of four main drift mixes, with a further insertion mix that was largely based on evergreen foliage, as a calmer contrast to the large-scale colourful flowering mixes (diagram 3).

Opposite top: In late summer and autumn the North American mix has another dramatic flowering, with the combination of blue *Aster macrophyllus* 'Twilight' and white *Aster divaricatus*. The division between the different mixes can still be clearly seen.

Opposite bottom: In late October, the seedheads of *Deschampsia cespitosa* create a hazy layer beneath the oak and beech woodland.

1.
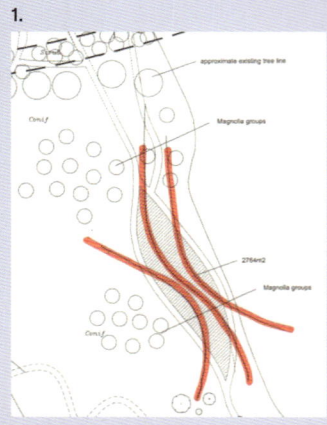

2.
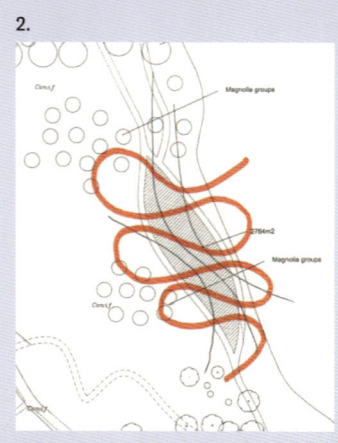

3.
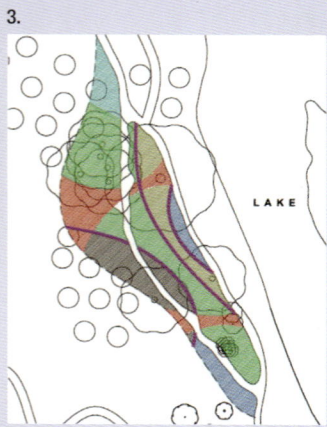

Top row: The lines separating out the different mixes are pegged out; these separating strips are planted with sedges, ferns and grasses; after the plants have been set out, the three mixes can be made out in flowing drifts.

Second row: This mix features pink and white forms of *Lamprocapnos (Dicentra) spectabilis*, which flower for several months. The foliage turns autumnal yellow in the summer.

Third row: This mainly blue, yellow and white mix is colourful in spring with primroses (*Primula vulgaris*), ferns, epimediums and pulmonarias. In early summer the white flowers of *Silene fimbriata* light up the shady spaces.

Bottom row: The North American mix in spring, with *Tiarella* 'Spring Symphony' and the striking bright fern fronds of *Dryopteris wallichiana* in one of the dividing strips; large repeating drifts of tiarella with scattered *Lamprocapnos spectabilis* 'Alba' and emerging clumps of green aster foliage; in early summer, the tiarella flowers are beginning to fade but the foliage of *Aster macrophyllus* 'Twilight' is growing up strongly around them. This is an example of the 'layering' principle of planting design.

Opposite: In winter, the aster seedheads have a dramatic presence, along the edge of one of the boundary strips of sedges, ferns and grasses.

ORDER IN CHAOS

For the rest of this chapter, we'll look at an organizational structure for naturalistic planting design. It's a method, a process that distils my own approach and thinking. I've developed this partly because I felt that a lot of the existing approaches were very confusing, had became bogged down in huge amounts of technical jargon, or didn't really fit with my own observations about how natural systems work. I've long felt that there's a need for a more straightforward way of tackling naturalistic planting design, one that does not require an advanced knowledge of plant science or ecology. It's also a response to my concerns that the 'randomized' approach to naturalistic planting design (or aspects of the technocratic strand), which is increasingly prevalent, is causing us to miss out on some of the most exciting and creative aspects of planting design – particularly the considered detail of plant association. As a result I see a need to bring together elements from all three of those strands that we discussed in the first chapter of the book.

We're going to start off with a metaphor. It's a conceptual framework that I come back to again and again. Partly that's because the methods we'll discuss in this chapter are intended to be universal – a set of principles and ideas that can be applied wherever you are. But it's mainly because it seems obvious that if we want to create a sense of nature, then we look to the laws of nature as a starting point. That's why I call it 'universal planting'.

We've all seen the amazing images that zoom in from a view of the Earth from space – continents, countries, regions and cities, right down to individual places. In fact, simply opening 'Google Earth' does exactly the same thing – going from space to your own back yard in a matter of seconds. Thinking at different scales gives you a fresh perspective, and enables you to see the bigger picture. So, in this spirit, let's expand the view even further!

Our planet is part of the solar system of planets that revolves around our star, the sun, which in turn links with other stars and planetary systems to form our galaxy, the Milky Way. In turn, a galaxy cluster is a structure that consists of anywhere from a few hundred to several thousands of galaxies, bound together by gravity, and these clusters can group together to form 'superclusters'. When you consider that an individual galaxy can consist of billions of stars, a galaxy supercluster represents organizational structure on a truly vast and incomprehensible scale.

You may be wondering what any of this has to do with planting design! The key point is in the previous sentence, 'organizational structure'. In our universe, the laws of nature apply everywhere, and they impose an organizational structure that operates across scales from the incredibly small to the unimaginably large. They establish a pattern or order on what at first might seem to be random chaos, and sometimes you need to be looking at the right scale to be able to detect that pattern. As we have seen in the preceding chapter, depending on the scale at which you are looking, different patterns become apparent, and when you are in any particular scale, it's very difficult to appreciate what's going on at the other scales.

What lies at the basis of all the different levels of organization across the entire reaches of space, from a collection of atoms to a galaxy supercluster, is gravity. According to the principles of physics, any object with a mass becomes a centre of gravity, and depending on the size or dominance of that object, other objects cluster around it, to greater or shorter distances. This idea of objects becoming centres of gravity lies at the basis of how I organize a planting.

UNIVERSAL FLOW

I call my method for naturalistic planting design 'Universal FLOW'. The universal part has two meanings: it signifies that this is a method that can be applied widely and is not restricted to certain parts of the world or to particular vegetation or planting types but instead is a set of principles that can be applied wherever you are; and it is also a metaphor for the whole process and set of ideas – we'll look at this shortly. FLOW is an acronym, made up of four separate components that each deal with a crucial element or elements in the planting design process: Forces and flow, Layers, Order, Waves.

- **Forces and flow** describes the factors operating on plants in any given area, and deals with the spatial, or horizontal, arrangement of plants.

- **Layers** refers to the vertical arrangement of plants and also the boundaries and divisions of spaces.

- **Order** is about how to create a sense of unity, coherence and legibility in plantings.

- **Waves** deals with the dynamics of planting, change over time, and management.

There's no order of priority where these components are concerned, but once each has been properly considered, then the planting scheme is complete.

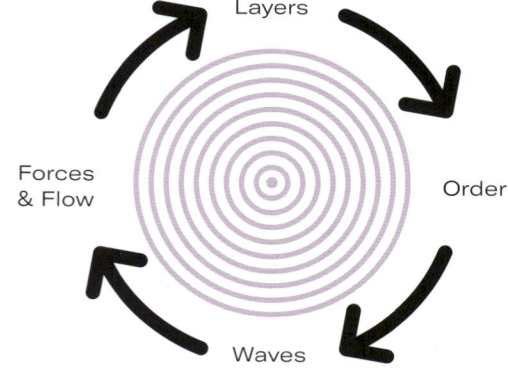

However, FLOW also describes the concept itself. The idea of flow, direction and movement is what makes a planting come alive; it's where I always start, since without it a scheme lacks energy and vitality. It's also a rationale for the spatial distribution of the plants in the scheme. Most guidance for naturalistic design is either for random planting or for a scattered distribution of the main structural, or 'emergent', plants. The question is, what dictates this scattered arrangement? Usually the answer is that there is no rationale behind it at all. But we do need to inject a sense of purpose into the planting, rather than relying on a random approach to establish the main framework.

Left: A detail from the author's 2013 gold-medal-winning Chelsea Flower Show garden with multi-layered eastern North American woodland planting. The plants are ecologically suited to be associated with each other, and are planted in a naturalistic mix, however, there is also a careful consideration of colour, texture and form. Pale blue woodland phlox, *Phlox divaricata* 'Clouds of Perfume' and white foam flower, *Tiarella cordifolia* 'Spring Symphony' in the foreground with pink *Geranium maculatum* 'Elizabeth Anne' punctuated by the taller emergent American columbine, *Aquilegia canadensis*, with contrasting red flowers, behind.

FORCES AND FLOW

In physics, a force is something that acts on an object and causes a reaction. In my FLOW planting design model, the concept of forces is how I think about the way different plants interact with each other in a scheme. Here we are going to consider in detail the spatial distribution of plants in a naturalistic scheme, and this in turn relates to the actual method of setting out and arranging plants.

Forces define the planting

The idea of forces acting on plants in any given location is the basis of plant ecology. Ecology is defined as 'the study of the interactions and relationships between, and among, living things and their environment'. These interactions have outcomes that lead to plant success or failure.

We can view these interactions and influences as the 'forces' that determine how plants grow in any one place. Understanding, and working with these forces is the essential starting point for planting design that is tuned to nature. This is why a fundamental evaluation of site conditions is the crucial first step in the planting design process: what are the forces that are acting on plants that are growing, or will be growing, in that location? Temperature, moisture level, pH, nutrient availability, exposure, and light level are just some of the physical 'forces' that will determine plant growth. Of course, we can amend the site to make those forces more benign to allow us to grow whatever we want, but the further we move away from the natural condition, the more energy will be needed to maintain those new conditions into the long-term.

It's not just external physical 'forces' that act upon plants but also the competitive interactions between plants that will also influence outcomes. Whether the forces are external to the planting, or internal, the Plant Strategy Theory (pages 100-103) provides a basis for understanding how diversity, co-existence and compatibility and can be maintained in different situations. Maintaining moderate stress and/or disturbance is the key.

The centres of gravity (COG) principle

Understanding the 'forces' that act on plants is the driving force for plant selection and it also drives consideration of how plants might be arranged. The COG principle describes the aggregated distribution of individuals of a plant species, and this is by far the most common plant distribution pattern. It's the 'cluster with outliers' arrangement, and I use it as the basis for building up a scheme. Instead of working on the principle that plant arrangement is random (as in the randomized planting method, or through the use of seed mixes), or that it occurs as arbitrary scatters or uniform drifts, think instead of centres of gravity. This is where the idea of forces comes in. Imagine the cluster of individuals of the same species being a centre of gravity, exerting an attractive force that weakens the further away you get from that centre. You will have a tighter grouping of plants at the core, which becomes more sparse the further you move away. This becomes the basic unit of planting. Then imagine that this centre of gravity not only attracts individuals of that same species, but also individuals of other species, which themselves will have that same cluster-with-outlier distribution. Combining the different species in a mix using this basic pattern will soon build up a complex series of interactions. The sequence of diagrams on page 111 show how this builds up.

It's all in the mix

When working with naturalistic plantings, we are in the main dealing with mixtures rather than with distinct groupings of individuals set out according to a rigid plan. We think in terms of the component species in a mix, and the proportional contribution of each species to the total. Typically I will use up to 20 species in any one mix – much more than this and things start to get too diluted.

Once I've established my line as the starting point, I'll then determine boundaries of the different mixes in the scheme. Using the idea of flow, the direction of these mixes will take the form of drift-like shapes that roughly follow the direction of the line. I'll use the principles of fuzzy edges and cross-overs to blur the boundaries between these mixes.

In the technocratic strand of naturalistic design, the plants in the mix would be planted randomly so as to get a truly spontaneous effect. I wish to have more control over plant associations within the mixtures, so I work a bit differently. In so doing, I need to think more generically about plant types.

We'll look at two main typologies: plant structural types and plant growth forms. These help us to decide on how to formulate and build up the detail of the planting as a whole and of the individual mixes.

Above: This planting at a factory site in the West Midlands was created through the use of a planting mix but no planting plan. In autumn, *Aster* 'Purple Dome' is prominent amongst structural grasses. The plantings are left to stand over winter, cut back in late January and then given a weed-over in spring.

Left: The mix was used on several nearby areas on the site and was composed carefully of different percentages of the component species to give the desired effect. Here, *Achillea* 'Moonshine' is in full flower in early summer.

Right: Later in the summer, kniphofias, white-flowering *Libertia formosa* and the green flowers of *Alchemilla mollis* make up the main display. The seed heads of the earlier flowering achillea are visible. Planting Design: Nigel Dunnett

Plant Structural Types

Landscape and garden designers differ in their classification of plant types, and those that follow are the ones I work with. They allow much more flexibility than some other classifications, and in the same way as the concept of building blocks, they are tuned to help build up a planting from a visual and structural viewpoint. Most of the planted area will be based on mixtures, rather than as a traditional planting plan. Where plants have fixed positions they will be shown on a plan, but otherwise it's the proportions of the different plants in the mix that need to be decided. This method is as much about how to go about arranging these plants on the ground as it is about making a plan.

I always think about how each individual species is distributed across the whole area, rather than visualizing them all together as a mass. It's how I work out the layering and the waves, or colour effects. So, when I set out a planting, I do it species by species, rather than filling in just one part of the planting with everything and then moving on to the next part. And I do that in the order of the plant types below: anchors, satellites and free-floaters.

Anchors

Anchor plants are the starting point, and they define the planting; I call them anchors because they are the fixed points around which everything else revolves. They are the centres of gravity, exerting the strongest pull. Without them the planting scheme would fall apart, so you need to have a clear idea about their placing. I use three different types of anchor plants, each of which has a different function.

a) Framework anchors are similar to the structural plants found in other designers' classifications. They have strong architectural forms and are used in relatively small numbers. They may be bold grasses or perennials as well as multi-stem trees or shrubs that make pillars, or columns, in the planting. Typically, they won't be part of any plant mixes, but will be located separately on a planting plan, forming an overlay on top of the pattern of mixes. I often use the S-shaped line to determine the scattering of these anchors (see page 111).

As noted, framework anchors generally sit outside of the individual mixes. However, all the other plant types below sit firmly within individual mixtures.

b) Matrix anchors form the glue that holds a scheme together. The matrix is an old idea in naturalistic planting – a lower layer in a planting through which taller plants can rise, but the matrix visually holds them in place. In meadow-like plantings, the matrix anchor plants are likely to be grasses. Typically they will be used in relatively large numbers, and will constitute part of the plant mixes that form the bulk of the planting. However, they need to be set out first, because their arrangement determines the positioning of everything else.

Above left: Framework anchors tend to be the star players in a planting and are used in relatively small numbers. Here, the fountaining African love grass, *Eragrostis curvula*, is a framework anchor plant within this field of Mediterranean annuals. The Garden House, Devon. Design: Keith Wiley

Above right: *Euphorbia characias* ssp *wulfenii* is a framework anchor plant in Beech Gardens at the Barbican, and was set out before the other plants when the plantings were implemented. Design: Nigel Dunnett

Above: Matrix anchor species tend to be used in larger numbers and do not necessarily have to be the star performers in a mix. They are often an essential starting point, however, because they provide the 'glue' that holds everything else together. In the perennial meadow at Trentham Gardens, the grasses *Stipa calamagrostis* and *Deschampsia cespitosa* are used as a matrix anchors. Here, *Stipa calamagrostis* is just starting to flower. Design: Nigel Dunnett

Left : The two grasses in the above planting being placed as matrix anchors, before any other species are placed around them.

Opposite: Early summer in the perennial meadow at Trentham Gardens. The matrix of the grasses is still visible before the main perennials begin their flowering.

Use grasses to anchor

Planting Design Toolkit

c) A character anchor is the essential starting point for a particular theme or character of a planting. It may not be a structural plant in the architectural sense; instead it may have a specific colour or form, or might typify the essence of a specific plant community.

The value of anchor plants is that not only do they give a structure and rationale to the planting, they also allow an element of plant association rather than randomized planting. You can use all three types of anchor in a single scheme, and also work with primary and secondary anchors that will form the basis of further plant associations within the mix. The scheme shown on page 111 works with a sequence of primary anchors and secondary anchors.

Top row: In the steppe plantings at the Barbican, two grasses were used as matrix anchors: blue moor grass (*Sesleria nitida*) flowering in the photos and blue oat grass (*Helicotrichon sempervirens*). As their names suggest, both these drought-tolerant grasses make a great contribution to the overall blue-green-grey appearance of these meadow-y plantings. Design: Nigel Dunnett

Bottom row: Matrix anchors do not need to be grasses. Here, the virtually evergreen narrow-leaved variegated perennial, *Pulmonaria* 'Cotton Cool' (which has blue flowers in spring) is used in the woodland garden at Trentham as a matrix within which clumps of the grass *Deschampsia cespitosa* can flower to create a hazy layer of flower above them. This combination, which also includes ferns and the variegated perennial forget-me-not, *Brunnera* 'Jack Frost', has visual appeal every day of the year. Design: Nigel Dunnett

Opposite: Matrix anchor species can be of any height. In the top picture, the very upright, robust grass, *Calamagrostis* x *acutiflora* 'Karl Foerster' is used as a matrix, with the lime yellow flowers of *Euphorbia palustris* flowering among the foliage clumps of the grass. In the same view later in the year (bottom picture), the grass is flowering, and the purple flowers of *Verbena bonariensis* and *Lythrum salicaria* combine with the blue of devil's bit scabious, *Succisa pratensis*. Design: Nigel Dunnett

Satellites

Next come 'satellite' species. These are the plants that coalesce around the anchors and provide the main character of the plantings at any one time. In terms of numbers of species, these will make up the majority of the planting. They will deliver the main visual interest and will provide continuity of flowering or other aesthetic value.

All of the above categories accord with the COG principle of a core grouping and outliers. I find the easiest way is to plant with 'units' of a single species: a clump of three plants, with one outlier, randomly distributed through the space. The scheme shown on page 111 uses this method. By starting off with your main anchor plants in this way and then moving sequentially to the satellites, you build up the planting species by species, gradually filling the space.

This page: In the Europe Garden of the 2012 London Olympic Park, the shasta daisy hybrid *Leucanthemum* x *superbum* 'T.E. Killin' (detail right) was used as a satellite species around the matrix grass *Stipa calamagrostis*. Design: Nigel Dunnett and Sarah Price

Right: *Lychnis chalcedonica* is the satellite species here in the perennial meadow at Trentham Gardens, within the matrix of *Stipa calamagrostis* and *Deschampsia cespitosa*. Design: Nigel Dunnett

Below: *Salvia nemorosa* 'Caradonna' is used as a satellite species here in Beech Gardens at the Barbican, around *Euphorbia characias* ssp. *wulfenii* Design: Nigel Dunnett

Planting Design Toolkit

Free-floaters

Free-floaters are the equivalent of 'fillers' in some of the other classification systems. They are gap-fillers and are another essential for the visual success of a scheme. There are essentially three types of free-floaters, all of which can be introduced at the end of the planting process and placed as appropriate in gaps and spaces.

a) Annuals and biennials; the former will die at the end of the growing season in which they have flowered, but may well self-seed into future years. They may be sown or planted into a scheme each year to add freshness and vitality or just used in the first year to fill gaps between permanent plants while they are still relatively small.

b) Short-lived perennials may be introduced as part of the scheme and may generate a substantial part of the initial visual interest. However, they may only be present for the first few years and then gradually die out, although some may self-seed.

c) Bulbs are essential early and mid-season performers, often providing the earliest flowering in a scheme and bursts of seasonal energy as later flowers push up through lower-growing plants.

Above: The California Bank at the London Olympic Park uses self-seeding California poppies, *Eschscholtzia californica*, to create dramatic displays on a hot south-facing bank. Design: Nigel Dunnett

Opposite Top: Many free-floating and ephemeral plants are used in the steppe meadow plantings at the Barbican. Here, *Allium* 'Globemaster' flowers in early summer, with the crimson flower heads of *Knautia macedonica*, and the bright pink flowers of heron's bill, *Erodium manescavii* just visible at the centre of the picture. The bulbs are distributed fairly uniformly through the plantings, and both the knautia and erodium are short-lived perennials that seed themselves around freely. Design: Nigel Dunnett

Opposite bottom: White *Lychnis coronaria* 'Alba' is another short-lived perennial, but it seeds itself, as does the bottle-brush-like steppe grass *Melica ciliata*. The allium seed heads remain a feature for much of the year. Design: Nigel Dunnett

Opposite Top: Alliums are used here at Great Dixter, Sussex as early flowerers among more bulky later-flowering perennials. *Aquilegia vulgaris* hybrids will seed freely among the plantings, as will the white sweet rocket, *Hesperis matronalis* 'Alba' behind.

Opposite Bottom: In the author's garden, annuals are used informally among permanent plantings. White monarch of the veldt (*Venidium fastuosum*) and purple cornflowers (*Centaurea cyanus* 'Black Ball') flower in between groups of perennial ornamental grasses, and white Bishop's flower (*Ammi majus*) fills in among taller plants behind.

Above: This seeded meadow containing many biennials and short-lived perennials for a temporary urban site aimed to capture some of the spirit of ephemeral species that colonize abandoned urban spaces. The seed mix was sown around the multi-stem specimens of Tibetan cherry, *Prunus serrula*. Prominent are the upright spikes of weld, *Reseda luteola*, that will re-seed itself once established. Design: Nigel Dunnett and Landscape Design Associates

Next page: The Stitch Meadows at the London Olympic Park use many free-floaters among more permanent, robust perennials. Examples here include, the purple *Dianthus carthusianorum* and the yellow daisies of *Buphthalmum salicifolium*. Design: Nigel Dunnett and James Hitchmough

Above: In the woodland garden at Trentham, white *Silene fimbriata* is a free-floating, short-lived perennial that seeds itself into gaps between more permanent species, such as the flowering perennial rhubarb, *Rheum palmatum atrosanguineum*.

Top left: A range of vertical forms in Beech Gardens at the Barbican with the strict uprights of the *Phlomis* seedheads, the tight verticals of *Miscanthus* 'Undine' and multi-stem *Prunus*, and the loose fans of the shorter grass, *Sesleria nitida*. The rounded forms of *Euphorbia wulfenii* make a strong contrast.
Top middle: In the author's garden, the strict upright *Miscanthus* 'Kleine Silberspinne' contrasts with the loose fountains of *Stipa calamagrostis*.
Top right: A strong contrast between the rigid upright *Calamagrostis* x *acutiflora* 'Karl Foerster' and the flat seed heads of *Achillea filipendulina*. Design: Dan Pearson

Centre left: The strict upright yellow phlomis, purple salvias and white libertias work nicely with the rounded form of the euphorbia in Beech Gardens. At the same time, the round allium flowers repeat the spherical whorls on the phlomis and round euphorbia flower heads.
Centre middle: Meadow-like plantings tend to be dominated by flat forms and verticals, such as here in the North American garden in the London Queen Elizabeth Olympic Park.
Centre right: A strong contrast here in the Stitch Plantings in the Olympic Park between the flat white flowers of wild carrot, *Daucus carota*, and the strictly vertical verbascums.

Bottom left: Repeated and widely spaced rounded forms are effective when standing out from a lower contrasting layer as here at the Barbican.
Bottom middle: Vertical 'emergents' ranging from strict to loose, in a lower textural matrix of the grass *Sporobolus heterolepis* in this Pennsylvania garden, USA.
Bottom right: Strongly contrasting textures and forms in the nut walk, Sissinghurst Castle, Kent.

Compatibility

An important reason for using the metaphor of forces for this section on spatial layout is that one of the main considerations in plant choice for naturalistic schemes is the idea of competitive compatibility. It's no use putting a mix of species together based on aesthetics alone, only for one or two of them to outcompete and dominate all the others. They need to be able to co-exist without the need for constant maintenance. In order to avoid undue competition in diverse mixes we need to do two things: first, ensure that there is moderate stress or disturbance in the system to deter the dominators and secondly, avoid selecting dominator-type plants in the first place.

I could go into great detail in terms of a functional classification of plants for design purposes, but in line with everything else in this book, I'm going to keep things as simple as possible. For me, there are just two main factors that need to be considered: reproduction capacity and growth rate. We can divide plants into three main types in this respect.
- Clonal or spreading plants are typical dominator types, and occupy space by colonizing adjacent areas through clonal growth.
- Clump-formers typically stay in the same place, forming tighter clumps, which of course may also become bigger over time.
- Seeders, which reproduce and spread.

In each of these categories, plants can also be divided into how aggressive or otherwise they are in their growth and reproduction: weak, moderate, and aggressive. Here are a few examples of how to use these ideas in composing plant mixes.

a) To create a diverse perennial meadow-like mix, I use mainly clump-formers with weak to moderate aggressiveness, mixed with some weak to moderate seeders and weak clonal species. All species showing aggressive character are to be avoided – they will be of the dominator type.

b) On very fertile or wetter sites, I am less wary of clonal or spreading species and use aggressive species that can fight it out with each other, together with robust clump-forming species.

c) For temporary schemes, or to create vibrant pop-up meadows, I use mostly seeders, perhaps with robust structural clump-formers planted among them.

Plant growth forms

There are many different ways of classifying plants according to their growth forms, but for design purposes, it's possible to divide them into just three main types:
- Upright
- Rounded
- Flat

We can further divide this according to how tall or short the plants are, and also how rigidly they adhere to these forms:
- Strict
- Moderate
- Loose

For example, a strict upright form would be a strong column, whereas a loose upright form might be more like a fountain.

There is no set formula for the proportions of different plant types to achieve a perfect outcome. However, for a meadow-like aesthetic, an excess of rounded forms will give a very lumpy appearance, and a majority of flat forms will offer a more naturalistic effect. Rounded and upright forms will give contrast, used in smaller numbers – large amounts of tall uprights, planted close together, will seldom be satisfactory. In very stressed situations, many durable-type plants will have a more rounded form, and these will look best if not too densely packed, with smaller numbers of upright and flat forms as contrast. It's useful to make simple sketches of the distribution of forms that you are aiming for in your planting, and then to use the plan to begin the search to put names against forms.

I repeat, there are no hard and fast rules about correct proportions of different types and forms to use in a naturalistic planting. Indeed, as I have hinted at before, where rules are given, they tend to be based on a relatively restricted set of grassland or meadow plant community types. If this book is about nothing else, it is about urging experimentation rather than following a set of rules – that's not the way that things work in the wild.

The best advice is to 'study the natural models'. Get to know what excites you and take that as your starting point. See what works in your climate zone and/or regional landscape. It's all about what does it for you, and how you then might wish to interpret that. What I hope is clear from the examples in this book is that contrast is essential – a complete uniformity of plant forms leads to a corresponding lack of visual interest.

CASE STUDY: OLYMPIC PARK STITCH PLANTINGS

Design: Nigel Dunnett
Implementation: Autumn 2012

The 'Stitch' plantings at the Olympic Park were designed to be a temporary solution that filled vacant plots prior to development and as highway-edge plantings to link the Olympic Park with surrounding neighbourhoods, evoking the character of the main park. It's a planting concept that mixes robust perennials, bulbs, and annuals/biennials to create low-cost but exuberant naturalistic mixes – a basic approach that I've worked with many times since, and it opens itself out to endless experimentation.

Below: Striking yellow spikes of foxtail lily, *Eremurus stenophyllus* and bright orange *Kniphofia triangularis*, with purple *Verbena bonariensis*, poke through the lower layers of annuals in early summer.

Top: In spring the annuals begin to flower, with early perennials such as *Papaver orientale*. The upright stems of *Verbena bonariensis* are prominent.

Above: These plantings are a combination of container-grown robust perennials, planted at relatively low density, bulbs, and a seed mix of annuals, biennials and short-lived perennials. All are established at the same time. Here perennials such as *Papaver orientale*, *Kniphofia* spp., *Foeniculum vulgare*, *Verbascum* 'Sixteen Candles' and *Perovskia atriplicifolia*, are mixed with bulbs such as *Allium* 'Globemaster'. The plants are established with a weed-free fine gravel or sand mulch, and the seed mix sown between the plants.

Planting Design Toolkit

Opposite: The annuals in full flower. I use 'slender annuals' such as these *Viscaria* hybrids that do not make large foliage rosettes and thus do not compete with the perennials.

Top and bottom left: As the annuals fade in summer, foxtail lilies (*Eremurus stenophyllus*) take over with flowering verbascums, kniphofias, and pink *Dianthus carthusianorum*.

Bottom right: Later in the summer, wild carrot, *Daucus carota* is abundant, with *Verbena bonariensis*.

Planting Design Toolkit

LAYERS

In traditional planting design the horizontal layout and arrangement of plants in a scheme is the whole story, but for us it might not even be the most important part. The concept of layers – the vertical structure and arrangement of plants and how they contribute to the visual impact of the planting – is of central importance. This is where we apply the concept of phenology. Layering and phenology has fascinated me for as long as I've been involved with planting design and it's a core aspect of the 'Sheffield' approach to planting.

However, when we talk about layers or canopies, this isn't the same thing as the layers in a cake, or a canopy in a forest, both of which are continuous solid entities that completely overtop the layer beneath. This might sometimes be the case, but it's not the way I think about it, and the inspirational wild examples don't really behave in this way. There's a danger in relying too much on a rigid vision of layers, and also of the idea of 'structural plants', because this encourages a sense that the planting is only complete at the end of the growing process, when these structural plants and all the layers are present, in place and fully formed. But when a planting is planned, the visual effect at all times must be borne in mind.

Instead, the layers are a lot more like a sieve, or a slab of cartoon cheese, full of holes. A series of eruptions or localized uprisings is a better way of thinking about it, rather than a uniform, homogenous layer. The phenology of the different plants in the mix can be used to generate the 'waves of colour' effect.

In the Europe Garden in the London Queen Elizabeth Olympic Park, the layers work like a series of eruptions or localized uprisings. Here, in May, the rounded forms and lime-green bracts of *Euphorbia palustris* are prominent in aggregated clumps and groupings. However, all of the lower green foliage around and between them belongs to other species that themselves will rise up to flower later in the year, in their own scattered and aggregated distributions, so that by the end of the summer, the euphorbia clumps will be completely hidden. Design: Nigel Dunnett and Sarah Price

Europe Garden, Queen Elizabeth Olympic Park

Design: Nigel Dunnett and Sarah Price
Implementation: 2012

Working with Sarah on the Europe Garden in the London Olympic Park enabled me to explore fully the concept of layering and phenology. The Europe Garden is part of a sequence of linear 'World Gardens' that run for 1km (⅔ mile) in length. They were all designed according to the same overall concept, with Sarah organizing the spatial structure of the gardens. The aim of the planting was to promote a very long season of visual delight as a result of lower layers rising up through the receding display of the earlier ones.

My concept for the Europe Garden was an evocation of a beautiful European hay meadow. I wanted to create the romantic feel and spirit of such a meadow, but to do it in an exaggerated way with abundant flowering, using species or cultivars that had a natural feel about them.

I used three anchor plants to give a framework to the planting: two matrix grasses, of which one, a relatively early flowerer, is *Deschampsia cespitosa* 'Golden Veil', and the other, a grass with impact later in the season, is *Stipa calamagrostis*. The other anchor plant is *Euphorbia palustris*, a plant of real character, which is a multi-season perennial that almost assumes the bulk of a shrub, with bright spring flowers, bold summer foliage and bright autumn colour. Groups of multi-stem hawthorn, *Crataegus monogyna*, create permanent structure, as do clipped evergreen hedges.

The garden is cut back to the ground in late winter, weeded over and mulched. The Europe Garden very neatly encapsulates my P3 rule – at any one time no more than three different plant species will dominate the visual effect of the planting.

Opposite: The euphorbias create a dramatic spring display before the main matrix grasses become dominant and later flowering species rise higher. Big clumps of foliage of one of these later species, *Cephalaria gigantea*, can be seen amongst the euphorbias.

Top left: The euphorbias have finished flowering, although the developing seed heads can still be seen, submerged among the rising foliage of later layers. Red *Lychnis chalcedonica* punctuates the green.
Top centre: The lychnis is now joined by white *Leucanthemum* x *superbum* 'T.E.Killin' and *Stipa calamagrostis* in flower, with yellow giant scabious, *Cephalaria gigantea*, producing the full 'stylized meadow' effect.
Top right: Great burnet, *Sanguisorba officinalis*, pokes through the eucantheum as it nears the end of its flowering time.

Middle left: The giant scabious rises to form a dramatic layer of its own.
Middle centre: Finally, in late summer, blue devil's bit scabious, *Succisa pratensis*, and purple loosestrife, *Lythrum salicaria* cultivars flower.
Middle right: *Stipa calamagrostis* ripens and stands through the winter, with the seed heads of *Cephalaria gigantea* emerging.

Bottom left: Overview of the Europe Garden in late October, with the seed heads of the grasses creating a feathery spectacle.
Bottom centre: The grass seed heads, and other plants with good structure, stand up through the winter.
Bottom right: The gardens are cut back in late January, and all the cuttings removed, to leave the evergreen hedges as permanent structure until the whole cycle of layers starts again.

Planting Design Toolkit

ORDER

I've discussed the vertical and horizontal spatial arrangement of plants, the dynamic qualities of plant layers and the choice of plant community models that are suitable for the site conditions that we have, or can manipulate. But that's not enough; it's important to inject a sense of legibility into naturalistic plantings so that there is an immediate sense of order and organization rather than random chaos. There are two ways that we can consider this: external order and internal order.

External order

We can create external order by considering design elements that occur outside the main detail of any particular planting. These elements might provide a strong contrast to the main naturalistic character, they might set a context to the planting, or they might frame it. The idea of framing a loose planting to give it a sense of strength and purpose and to emphasize its naturalness is an important one. Partly it goes back to the Picturesque idea of creating pictorial impressions, and the framing of those pictures can be as crucial as the contents themselves. Almost by definition, these external elements will have an architectural quality, whether very formal or completely informal.

Above: Repetition of formal columns and mounded shapes creates order and legibility among the looser perennial and grass plantings in the Italian Garden at Trentham. Design: Tom Stuart-Smith

Left: Lines of regularly spaced hazels (*Corylus avellana*) and the straight stone path give organization and order to what will be a gloriously naturalistic perennial ground layer in spring and summer.

Top: Clipped linear hedges give order and sense to a more naturalistic woodland canopy above, and create smaller more intimate spaces in this pocket park near City Hall, London. Design: Townsend Landscape Architects

Bottom left: A formal avenue of trees behind, clipped hedges, regular steps, and clumps of large shrubs frame and contain the more informal perennial plantings in the Southern Hemisphere Garden in the London Queen Elizabeth Olympic Park. Design: Sarah Price and James Hitchmough

Bottom right: Voluptuous and exuberant planting is contained and framed within more formal circular beds separated by paths, and clipped beech (*Fagus sylvatica*) hedges within the plantings, at RHS Wisley, Surrey. Design: Tom Stuart-Smith

Planting Design Toolkit

Asia Garden, Queen Elizabeth London Olympic Park

Design: Nigel Dunnett and Sarah Price
Implementation: 2012

Each of the four world gardens at the Olympic Park had the same structure and components. These consisted of the field plantings (layered naturalistic perennial plantings designed by myself and James Hitchmough); the strips (monocultural linear blocks of architectural perennials and grasses); and the hedges (formally clipped evergreen box hedges). The overall design of the gardens and the spatial structure of the hedges and strips were set out by Sarah. Without this structure to contain them, the field plantings would potentially have little legibility and might tend towards an undefined free-form character. The evergreen hedges in particular give a great sense of solidity, permanence and 'line' against the naturalistic field plantings, and they set each other off.

While the other three World Gardens in the London Olympic Park were designed to be floral spectacles, my concept for the Asia Garden was to be a complete contrast to these. Of course there would be flowers, but there would be an equal emphasis on foliage textures and contrasts to create a more calming impression. My reference point for this garden was the beautiful wildflower meadows that I had seen in China with irises and thalictrums. Species lilies provided ephemeral drama, and hostas, *Persicaria amplexicaulis* and Japanese anemones were located in lightly shaded areas. In place of the diverse complex mixtures of the other World Gardens, I created Japanese anemone 'swathes' that would create uplifting flowering in late summer and autumn, interplanted with a matrix and ground-cover grasses. But it is the bold strips of very upright and structural grasses that define this garden, and which elevate it beyond a simple naturalistic scheme. They are *Calamagrostis* x *acutifolia* 'Karl Foerster', and the *Miscanthus sinensis* cultivars 'Flamingo', 'Silberfeder' and 'Gracimillus'.

Below: Swathes of Japanese anemone, *Anemone* x *hybrida* cultivars, between blocks of upright *Calamagrostis* x *acutiflora* 'Karl Foerster'.

Top left: The naturalistic plantings in the Asia garden give a flavour of the diverse wildflower meadows found in Sichuan and Yunnan, China.
Top right: Large blocks of the grass *Calamagrostis* x *acutiflora* 'Karl Foerster' create a strong sense of order among the naturalistic plantings in the Asia Garden in July.

Middle left: The same view in January, with the structural grasses remaining (*Calamagrostis brachytricha* is prominent) along with the curving evergreen box hedges.

Middle right: The mauve flowers of *Hosta* 'Tall Boy' with the flower spikes of *Thalictrum delavayi* 'Album' and multi-stem Chinese birch, *Betula albo-sinensis* in the Asia garden.

Bottom left: Purple flowers of the Yunnan thalictrum, *Thalictrum delavayi* mixed with the white form, *Thalictrum delavayi* 'Alba'.
Bottom right: Strong textural and structural contrasts between the blocks and clumps of grass, and the formal clipped box hedge in the Asia garden.

The Diamond Garden, Buckingham Palace
Design: Nigel Dunnett
Implementation: 2013

The Diamond Garden was installed to commemorate Queen Elizabeth's 60th anniversary of her accession to the British throne: the Diamond Anniversary. The garden is in the public realm outside the Queen's Gallery, and is the main drop-off point for tourists visiting the palace. There was a complex design brief: diamond symbols had to be included; maintenance was to be very simple; the gardens needed to look good every day of the year; overall the vegetation had to be relatively short to prevent any danger of explosive items being hidden as a counter-terrorism precaution; the flowering plants had to have proven value to pollinating insects – and all this had to work under the shade of mature London plane trees.

The garden is based on a regular square grid, turned 90 degrees to create diamonds, and then stretched to give a strong sense of perspective and depth. The grid is picked out with Portland limestone strips – a bright, creamy white stone that looks good throughout the year. Within the grid there are two types of planting. A strongly naturalistic, meadow-like planting with pink, purple and white colours fills the majority of the space. To contrast strongly with this, a smaller number of 'cells' are filled with mostly evergreen groundcovers. The flowering of the garden happens mostly in the spring and early summer, then it cools down to a tapestry of foliage patterns in the summer shade. This patterning stays in place through the autumn and winter.

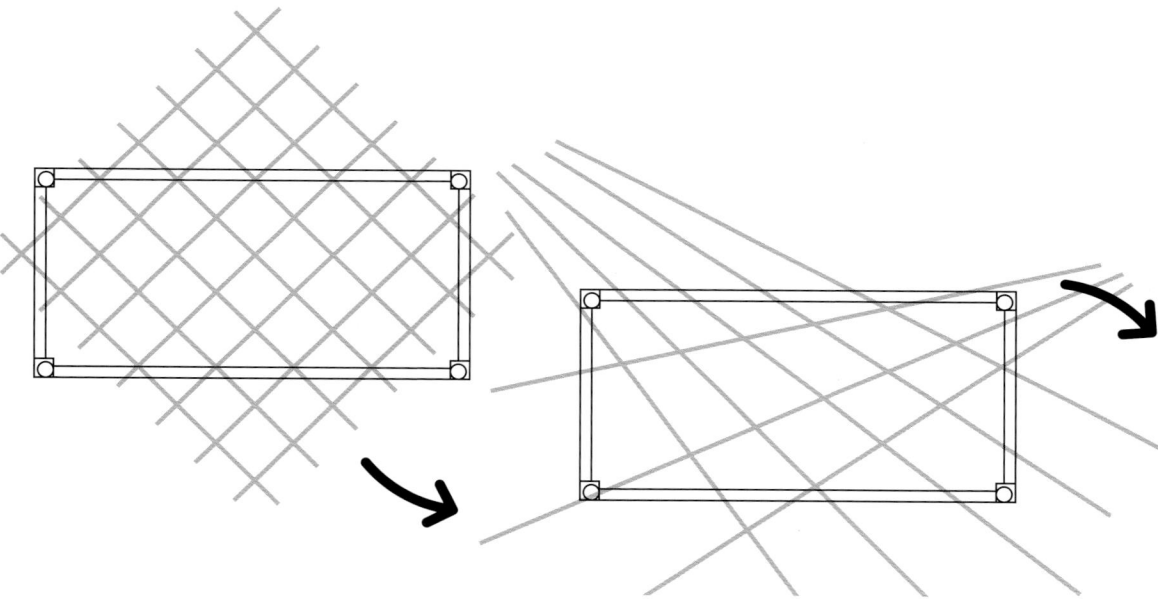

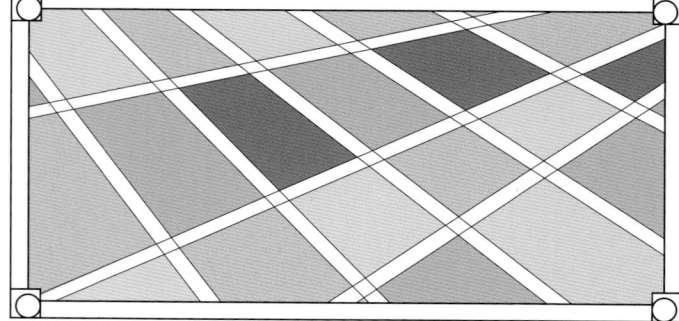

Above: The garden was installed to commemorate the Diamond Jubilee of Queen Elizabeth II, and reference to diamond forms was a requirement in the brief for the design. This author developed the concept by first creating a simple grid of squares to fit over the site, and then rotating this by 45 degrees to create a repeating pattern of diamonds. This grid was then stretched at one end in both directions to create flattened and elongated shapes, which also gave a strong sense of perspective. In turn, this network was translated into a series of 'cells' for planting, separated by stone strips that also functioned as exploratory internal paths.

Top row: Construction of the diamond strips (left) and starting to set out plants in the 'cells' (right).

Middle row: The garden soon after planting in June 2013 (left) and looking along the strips in early summer, with wood rush, *Luzula sylvatica*, flowering (right).

Bottom left: From late summer onwards in this dry shade garden, a tapestry of foliage forms the main visual interest and, because most species are evergreen, lasts through the winter. The grey-infused leaves of *Brunnera macrophylla* 'Jack Frost' are prominent here.

Bottom right The established garden, with white *Geranium × cantabrigiense* 'St Ola' and pink *Geranium macrorrhizum* 'Pindus'.

The straight line and the curve

Up to now, nearly everything I've written about has involved flowing shapes and a strongly organic underlying structure. I definitely stand by that as the starting point for naturalistic design, but when it comes to order and framing, then straight lines and a more formal geometry do of course have their place. The Buckingham Palace example is just one instance of that.

Rather than starting out with that rigidity and formality, unless a strongly formal scheme is desired I often prefer to superimpose the formal geometry afterwards, as a sort of intervention to the predominantly naturalistic structure. I will always lean towards the flowing form and the sense of mystery and drawing in of the viewer, but the idea of intervention is to provide a counterpoint that heightens that naturalistic character even further.

Internal order

While external order concerns factors that frame or give larger scale organization to space, internal order concerns factors that give organization, definition, and a strong sense of purpose to the planting itself. This is where we make decisions that turn a naturalistic assemblage of plants from a chaotic and random mix, to one which can be read, understood, and appreciated at a glance. It's what the term 'legibility' is all about.

It's crucial to the success of a scheme, and we've already discussed a lot of potential ordering factors already in this chapter. Many of these come within the realm of standard or traditional planting design practice: form, line and texture but there are several that are more closely linked with how natural plant communities work: rhythm and repetition of elements, and the value of emergents, for example. There are also ordering factors that are unique to an ecological aesthetic and that relate to 'fitness to site' and the complementarity of plant adaptations that make species from similar habitats work in harmony with each other. The photos on page 103, showing plant communities growing in very stressed habitats given an indication of this.

There is however, one elements that we haven't looked at so far: it's now time to delve into the world of colour.

Top: The repeated geometric shapes of the architecture and the round forms of the stairwell entrances at the Barbican, London, contrast strongly with the looseness of the planting. Planting Design: Nigel Dunnett

Left: In the author's garden, regularly spaced wave-form log piles, give permanent structure within the naturalistic plantings, and also have high biodiversity value. Within the plantings, geometric paths foster an immersive experience.

Above: There is a wonderful contrast between the sense of order created by the circular terraces in this amazing semi-amphitheatre in the Scott Arboretum at Swarthmore College near Philadelphia, USA and the much more random and natural distribution of the tall tulip trees (*Liriodendron tulipifera*) within it.

Left: The regular and quite formal distribution of the multi-stem river birch (*Betula nigra*), and their relatively uniform shapes, makes a striking contrast with the much more free-form character of the meadows beneath. This contrast and sense of order magnifies the exuberant naturalness of the meadow.

Colour

For me, colour is fundamental. We can work with everything discussed so far and develop an amazing planting scheme, but to me, carefully chosen colour can lift the scheme to another level entirely. It's not something that everyone agrees with – many people in the naturalistic planting world consider colour to be a secondary consideration to form and structure. But, coming back to the earlier discussion of the various strands in naturalistic planting design, colour is central to the impressionistic tradition, and it's something that I'm keen to bring back in as a driving factor in naturalistic design.

There's a huge amount of information available on traditional colour theory – harmony, contrast, the colour wheel and so on – and I won't repeat that here. It's good as a starting point, but it's important not to get stuck in a rut of 'tastefulness'. The naturalistic aesthetic opens itself out to experimentation and boldness. I look to artists for colour inspiration, and in particular to modernist art, where colour combinations can be exciting and unexpected. Like many, I'm naturally drawn to the Impressionists, and many people say that my plantings are like impressionistic paintings, drawn in the landscape. But I also find the more abstract, surreal and expressionist work of Paul Klee to have an overwhelming relationship with meadow-like forms, and the colour combinations can be extraordinary.

This page: A colour-themed annual seed mix at Trentham Gardens uses pinks, purples and blues with a small dash of contrasting orange. When working with colour, I aim for harmonious colours with a small amount of a strong contrasting colour to highlight. Seed mix design: Nigel Dunnett

Opposite: Three plants with similar and complementary flower shapes, but contrasting colours: *Echinacea purpurea*, *E. pallida* and a silver eryngium in the gardens at Dove Cottage Nursery, Yorkshire.

Top left: The planted perennial meadow at Trentham Gardens employs a strong colour scheme of whites, purples, blues and pinks for its main display period. **Top right:** *Leucanthemum* x *superbum* 'Becky', *Verbena bonariensis*, *Nepeta* 'Dawn to Dusk' and *Achillea* 'Summer Wine'. Design: Nigel Dunnett.

Middle left: A small touch of yellow from *Achillea* 'Gold Plate' gives a hint of contrast, and the billowing meadowsweet, *Filipendula ulmaria*, provides texture. **Middle right:** *Malva moschata* 'Alba' with *Salvia nemorosa* 'Caradonna' and *Knautia macedonica*.

Bottom left: Repetition of colour and form adds to the visual drama. In the foreground, *Eupatorium* 'Purple Bush' is emerging and will create a layer later in the summer. **Bottom right:** *Leucanthemum* x *superbum* 'Becky' with *Verbena bonariensis* and *Eupatorium* 'Purple Bush'.

Opposite: Planting at the University of Vienna Business School campus designed by Zaha Hadid complements the strong colour of the building. Blue nepeta lines the path edges with dark blue *Salvia nemorosa* 'May Night' behind. Design: BUSarchitecktur & BOA

Top left: The pale yellow flower spikes of both *Phlomis fruticosa* and *Sisyrinchium striatum* work well with the more rounded lime-green bracts of *Euphorbia characias* ssp. *wulfenii*. Planting Design: Nigel Dunnett

Top right: Plants in this hot scheme include red *Crocosmia* 'Emberglow' and yellow *Achillea* 'Paprika' with blue *Salvia nemorosa* 'Caradonna' for contrast. Although plant heights are similar, there is a wide range of textures and forms from the gently arching grass, *Melica ciliata*, to the strongly upright *Kniphofia* 'Tawny King'.

Middle left: This colour-themed meadow seed mix focus on brilliant shimmering white with a hint of pink, lifted by splashes of purple. The mix includes hedge bedstraw (*Galium mollugo*), yarrow (*Achillea millefolium*), oxeye daisy (*Leucanthemum vulgare*) and great knapweed (*Centaurea scabiosa*). It's an example of using, in this case, native British species, but combining them in ways that never occur in the wild.

Middle right: The pinks and purples of the echinaceas (*E. pallida* and *E. purpurea*) harmonize with the blue of *Aster macrophyllus* 'Twilight' while yellow solidagos, *Echinacea paradoxa* and *Rudbeckia fulgida deamii* provide contrast. The upright forms of the echinaceas with their downward drooping flowers associate well with the more rounded form of the asters. The vertical green-blue grass, *Andropogon geradii* prevents an otherwise 'flat' perennial planting and the multi-stemmed crab apples give essential structure and framing to the planting. Design: Sarah Price and James Hitchmough

Bottom left: This mainly recessive mix of greens, yellows and pale pinks is enlivened by the repetitive patches of *Bergenia* 'Rotblum' in the woodland garden at Trentham. Design: Nigel Dunnett

Bottom right: This 'steppe meadow' seed mix in the Olympic Park is suited to hot dry places. The mix was carefully colour balanced to focus on blue shades, pink and purple. Here, viper's bugloss *Echium vulgare* flowers with flax, *Linum perenne*, giant scabious, *Centaurea scabiosa*, and squirrel grass, *Hordeum jubatum*. Within this harmonious colour mix there are strong contrasts in the form and textures of the different component plants, giving rise to great visual interest. Seed mix design: Nigel Dunnett

Transparency

A very useful and subtle way to introduce internal order is through the idea of transparency. Transparent plants have height and structure, but allow views through. Many grasses that form low foliage clumps but throw up fountains of flower heads fall into this category.

Transparent plants can work in the same way as framing elements – by placing these taller yet see-through plants closer to the viewer, a sense of foreground and depth is produced.

Above: Transparency plays an important role in the perennial meadow at Trentham. The ability to see through plants is something that just isn't possible with traditional planting design where taller plants go at the back and shorter plants go at the front. Here, the grasses *Deschampsia cespitosa* and *Stipa calamagrostis* catch the low sun, with *Verbena bonariensis*, *Knautia macedonica*, *Nepeta* 'Dawn to Dusk', *Leucanthemum* x *superbum* 'Becky', *Lychnis coronaria* 'Alba' and *Malva moschata* 'Alba'. Design: Nigel Dunnett

Overleaf: These sheets of blue *Scilla messeniaca* at Sissinghurst Castle, Kent beneath witch hazels are highlighted and enhanced by the small amount of white *Anemone appenina*. Although still dramatic, the blue would have less impact without the touches of white.

WAVES

I referred earlier to the concept of waves of colour being the basis of how I think about the visual effect of my plantings over time. Let's think about this a bit more. The physical definition of a wave is that it's an oscillation or vibration that transmits energy through space, and it's the perfect metaphor for this type of planting: oscillations or fluctuations around a point or line which is relentlessly moving forward, but at any one point on that line there's a surge or sequence of effects. The plantings at the Barbican, London, were based upon this principle.

Managing dynamic naturalistic plantings

This wave analogy can be extended to much longer periods of time than a single year and used as the basis for how we think about longer-term management. The idea of change and development over time is one of the most difficult concepts to communicate to people when it comes to this type of planting: it's so different to the standard landscape and garden practice, which is much more static and usually about maintaining plantings to keep them looking the same from one year to the next.

Above left: The concept of dynamic management, as opposed to static maintenance, can be a difficult one to grasp. As well as a standardized programme of annual maintenance operations, there is also the need for informed management decisions so that diversity and character is maintained. As well as routine annual 'editing', this might mean substantial reworking every five to ten years to redress the balance between overly competitive plants, or to replace some elements that might have disappeared.

Above right: 'Designed plant communities' have many of the characteristics of naturally occurring plant communities. These include internal regeneration and seeding. For example, in the steppe meadows at the Barbican, there are many short-lived 'pop-up' plants and self-seeders. These will move around from year to year, filling gaps and dying-out. Maintenance can still be relatively simple, but it also needs to be knowledgeable and informed, requiring on-the-spot decisions about what to take out, what to move, and what to leave; and the ability to recognize what is desirable and what is a weed. Much can be achieved by developing maintenance manuals for specific projects, and also through training events for gardeners.

Managing the sort of naturalistic plantings that this book is devoted to is largely about maintaining diversity, or to put it in another way, about preventing dominance by undesirable species. Generally, if you leave an area of planting alone, over time the natural processes of succession (the directional change in a plant community from a starting point) will take hold. Succession will completely change the character and content of that vegetation, and will generally result in a long-term decrease in diversity. But over shorter time periods, there will be much fluctuation in abundance of different species in a mix. Those fluctuations may be minute or they may be extreme. The role of the gardener is to steer these fluctuations to maintain the plantings as closely as possible to the 'line of travel'.

When we work with the plant community approach, we work with plant mixes. These are subject to change, and individuals of species may move around in the space. That's what being dynamic is all about. And so from the outset we need to have a vision about how we want that planting to develop, and what operations are required to achieve that. The question of course is what this vision is. It's highly likely that the actual detailed balance and composition of the mixes will change, but does the vegetation retain the visual 'essence' of the desired community? This is where the idea of anchor species is important, because you have already decided which species are the cornerstones or foundations of the planting, there will be a desire to retain these in roughly the same proportions.

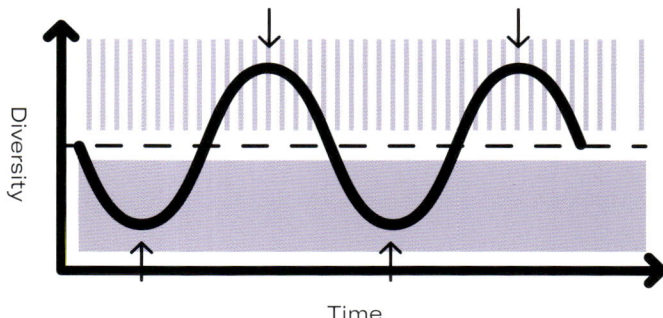

Time

The concept of steering the planting revolves around these interventions that push things in a certain direction, and then further interventions may well be needed to steer it back.

By using the FLOW method, and by considering all the different elements within it, it is possible to create plantings that are beautiful, uplifting and tuned to nature. They will be sumptuous, calming, enriching and joyful to experience. But the aesthetics is only one part of their value: how they look only tells a fraction of the story. In the next chapter we'll see how these types of plantings can have tremendous environmental impact too.

Above: Diagram to show how using the concept of waves gives us a conceptual framework for dynamic management of naturalistic plantings. Let's say that the dotted line represents the desired character and diversity of the plantings. The black line represents change in diversity and character over time. When the line dips into the flat mauve area, then diversity is decreasing, for example through dominance of the plantings by one or two very aggressive and competitive species. When the line rises into the broken mauve area then diversity is increasing, perhaps through weed invasion or self-seeding of individuals in the planting, and the desired character and prominence of key species is being diluted through sheer numbers of individuals of other plants. The arrows represent maintenance interventions that push the plantings back in the desired direction, and remove the dominating or overwhelming effect of undesired species.

Above: White *Ammi majus* and mauve *Viscaria oculta* in a colour-themed annual meadow mix on an urban site in Sheffield. Seed Mix design: Nigel Dunnett

Generally we will be aiming to maintain a certain level of ecological and visual diversity in the plantings. As a result the main objective of dynamic management is to intervene to steer the plantings along a line of travel so that diversity and character are maintained. The converse of maintaining diversity is to prevent dominance by undesirable or unwanted species. The diagram above gives an example of how using the concept of waves gives us a conceptual framework for dynamic management of naturalistic plantings. Let's say that the dotted line represents the desired character and diversity of the plantings. The black line represents change in diversity and character over time. When the line dips into the flat mauve area, then diversity is decreasing, for example through dominance of the plantings by one or two very aggressive and competitive species. When the line rises into the broken mauve area then diversity is increasing, perhaps through weed invasion or self-seeding of individuals in the planting, and the desired character and prominence of key species is being diluted through sheer numbers of individuals of other plants. The arrows represent maintenance interventions that push the plantings back in the desired direction, and remove the dominating or overwhelming effect of undesired species.

FUTURE NATURE

Our future is uncertain, hugely challenging and potentially catastrophic, with global climate change, increasing urbanization and scarcity of resources. All of these will in some way have an impact on everyone. In fact, we are already familiar with the implications of these challenges: severe urban flooding and the urban heat island effect; air and water pollution; social and health problems; elimination of biodiversity and lack of contact with nature. All of these and more are magnified out of all proportion in our towns and cities because have lost the soils, vegetation and wildlife from these areas. As a result, we lack the soil and plant layer that acts like a sponge, soaking up excess stormwater; prevents the heating up of all the urban hard surfaces; filters dirty air and water; and provides us with the contact with nature that is crucial for our effective functioning. Instead we have the dominance by hard surfaces that absorb and reflect heat, shed rainwater and are hostile to life.

A RADICAL APPROACH

When you look at things in this way, it becomes clear that the answer to addressing these challenges is to put back, on a large scale, the soils, wildlife and vegetation into our cities and surroundings. That sounds straightforward, but the opportunities for creating extensive new areas of traditional 'greenspace' and gardens may be limited on the ground in existing urban areas. Instead, we must be radical and consider all those places that even a short while ago would have been viewed as outside the scope of mainstream horticulture. They include rooftops, walls, pavements, car parks, streets, business parks and commercial developments.

I have long seen this environmental agenda as one of the most exciting future avenues for garden and landscape design, particularly planting design (these opportunities only work because of the interactions between plants and soil). When this is done in visible and accessible locations where people will be seeing, using, and enjoying them, that means gardens, landscapes, ecology and horticulture – exactly what this book is about! But the sad fact is that, with only a few exceptions, the full potential of planting design has yet to be applied in these situations. This is partly because where a feature, garden or space is deemed to have a strongly ecological function, there is huge pressure for the character to be fundamentally 'ecological' too, and for the planting to be confined to native plants. These projects have been seen as mainly the realm of the engineer and ecologist, and although they are based on vegetation and nature, notions of aesthetics have been regarded as of relatively little importance.

Above and right: Green Infrastructure is the interconnected network of soils and vegetation within an urban context. Here on a main street in Singapore, traffic can be glimpsed beneath the cooling canopy of street trees, while at ground level, epiphytes grow on the tree trunks, 'living columns' repeat along the street, and rocks are placed beneath trees. This comprehensive inclusion of living and natural forms in the everyday environment is core to the concept of 'biophilic' design.

Previous page: The dominance of hard surfaces, and the absence of soils and vegetation, magnifies the future challenges of an extreme and highly variable climate.

Above: This neighbourhood in the Chinese city of Chongqing has a generous network of shade trees filling the spaces between apartment blocks, while all the roof surfaces are used for recreational space and food-growing.

However, this offers a huge opportunity to take exciting planting designs and extend them from traditional application in parks and gardens to new and challenging locations in the heart of the modern city – in other words, to open up new possibilities and markets for horticulture and creative ecological design. This is the reason I have been so active at bringing these ideas into the wider public imagination through show garden designs at the RHS Chelsea Flower Show and through the work of the RHS 'Greening Grey Britain' campaign, of which I've been the Ambassador. Increasing amounts of research support the assertion that the type of planting that this book is all about (diverse, multi-layered, long-season, low-input, suited to site, floriferous plant communities) delivers maximum benefit, rather than 'native-ness' in itself. By working in this way we create wildlife-friendly, biodiverse environments that are teeming with life.

Opposite and above: We have to take over spaces previously considered of no horticultural or ecological value. Scott Weber's sidewalk planting in Portland, Oregon, USA shows what huge unrealized potential there is.

Top: The sheer diversity of planting and visual interest in this water-sensitive scheme of rain gardens in Sheffield has transformed the street for both people and wildlife. Planting design: Nigel Dunnett and Sheffield City Council

So, let's make environmentally friendly gardens and landscapes go mainstream by designing them to be the most exciting and beautiful types of planting there are. They're exciting because there are so many points of interest behind them, beyond how attractive they look. They're multi-functional – everything serves additional purposes beyond the aesthetic, whether it's providing for pollinators, improving microclimates, cutting air pollution, or dealing with too much or too little rainfall. It makes a garden or landscape so much more interesting. One of the most exciting aspects of a multi-functional viewpoint is that it breaks down the separations between the built and vegetative environments and sees everything as part of a whole system. Nowhere is this more apparent than when we consider the use of water in the inhabited landscape.

When it comes down to it, global environmental and climate change is mediated by water – too much of it leading to damaging and even catastrophic flooding, while too little creates drought conditions, extreme water shortages and water-use restrictions. In the former case we need to develop planted landscapes that will soak up that extra rainwater like a sponge and in the latter we must look to new planting methods that do not need irrigation or watering but still look fantastic.

RAIN GARDENS AND WATER-SENSITIVE DESIGN

While the term 'rain garden' is evocative and exciting in itself, the concept is even more so: the use of garden and landscape features that collect, clean, store and slowly filter rainwater runoff back into the ground following severe rain-storms. It's an idea that is absolutely of the moment as climate change becomes an ever-present reality, and it elevates gardens from the purely decorative to something that can make a genuine contribution to reducing the seriousness of flash-flooding.

Rain gardens take the form of depressions or lower areas in the garden or landscape that can temporarily fill up with water that then drains away again. If the existing soil is free-draining this might be sufficient, but where the soils and geology are impermeable or poorly draining, additional drainage may be required, and a gritty growing medium or substrate used instead of the naturally occurring soil. Linear features that can move water through the garden or landscape are known as 'swales' or 'bioswales'. Both rain gardens and bioswales are constructed using exactly the same principles. In the UK, the use of landscape and gardens to manage stormwater is generically called by the hugely uninspiring term 'sustainable drainage systems (SuDS)'. It's an engineering-led term that I try not to use, much preferring the term 'water-sensitive design' that holds sway elsewhere.

Water-sensitive design may be the only basis of complete gardens and landscapes, and there is a lot of technical information available about how to do it. However, the one element that has received very little attention is the actual planting itself. That's surprising, given that it's the most visible part and it's the planting, in combination with the soil, that actually makes these features work.. But it's a tricky thing – plants need to be able to tolerate periodic inundation, but must also deal with the dry periods in between. Rain gardens have suffered in the past from what seems to be an almost inevitable assumption that because they have an ecological function, the only types of plants that will work properly are natives. Of course, that's not the case at all, but it has really limited the creative planting aspect of water-sensitive design.

So, we'll take a look at some examples of my own where I've attempted to demonstrate the huge potential for the planting designs of rain gardens. I haven't gone into any depth here in terms of technical details: the purpose is to show the way in which I've designed the planting. Typically I will use many plants that might originally come from wet meadows, the margins of wetlands or flood plain sites for the lowest areas in a rain garden or swale, while slightly higher up I will choose robust meadow and prairie-type plants that can tolerate some drying out. Around the edges of the features the plants might well be quite drought-tolerant because they will rarely be affected by rainwater inundation.

My front garden

The reason I became interested in the rain garden idea many years ago is that I could see the potential for using this and other small- to medium-scale garden and landscape features as a means of introducing beautiful and biodiverse plantings, often into places that previously might have been grim and grey.

I wrote a book on the subject (*Rain Gardens*, Timber Press, 2007) and designed a number of Chelsea Flower Show gardens between 2011 and 2013 that were based on the rain garden idea. So when I moved to a new house, I decided to convert the front garden into a demonstration of a rain garden. But I wanted this to be a different type of rain garden: if you do a google image search for 'rain gardens', most of the results show informal, amoeboid shapes, often surrounded by lawn. It seems that where a garden or landscape feature has an ecological function such design approaches nearly always ensue. Instead, I wanted to take a more formal approach to indicate that these ideas will work in all sorts of settings. Above all, I aimed to investigate the potential of dynamic, long-season plantings as the basis for rain garden design.

Originally the garden sloped away from the house, with no central path from the front gate. I terraced the garden, using dry-stone retaining walls, and put in a straight path, on a diagonal, from the front gate. This central path is flanked on both sides by linear swales. Apart from taking run-off from the path (which is permeable in that it is not set into mortar or pointed between the pavers, thereby allowing water to filter through), the main purpose of the swales is to absorb run-off directly from the roof of the house.

Above: The author's front garden shortly after construction was completed. The narrow plantings along each side of the main path function as linear bioswales, receiving rain-water runoff from the house roof and the path. They were deliberately created as rectangular shapes to demonstrate that ecological features can work equally well in formal geometric layouts as well as in informal organic designs.

Disconnect your downpipes!

The mantra of the rain garden movement is 'Disconnect your downpipes!' Instead of channelling water from the roof into the main drainage system, that water is diverted into the landscape. The theory is that if sources of run-off to the main drainage system are reduced, overloading of the system and subsequent flooding pressure downstream is reduced too. At my own home, I cut off two of the plastic downpipes at their base and, using standard connectors and guttering lengths from the local DIY store, continued the pipes through the garden to the beginning of the swales.

The main planting took place in the spring of 2014. The planting concept was to use successional layers to create a continuous flowering display from spring through to autumn, and then to have a good winter structure of stems and seed heads. Planting design for rain gardens and swales is not straightforward, because the vegetation has to deal with extreme dry periods as well as periodic influxes of water, and the sloping nature of the edges of both rain gardens and swales means that the base will stay relatively moist for longer periods, while the higher areas might dry out completely. A mix of plants is therefore advisable to cope with these conditions, placing those with the greatest tolerance of wetter conditions at the base.

The main flowering period in my garden is between midsummer and early autumn, and is built around the quartet of Astilbe chinensis var. taquetii 'Purpurlanze', Lythrum salicaria 'Zigeunerblut', Rudbeckia fulgida var. deamii and Crocosmia x crocosmiiflora 'George Davison', with a range of other species playing a supporting role. Amid this purple and gold extravaganza, the soft lilac-blue flowers of the native devil's bit scabious (Succisa pratensis) weave their way through the more solid framework players. A little earlier in the year, the upright spikes of Ligularia 'The Rocket' match the rising vertical flower stalks of the astilbe, followed by the acid yellow of Hemerocallis 'Whichford' complementing the astilbe's purple blooms. Before that, the ghostly lavender flowers of Iris 'Mrs Rowe' emerge among the expanding foliage of the later-flowering species.

Top left and centre: the downpipes from the house roof were disconnected from the drains and diverted and extended to outflow into the bioswales.

Top right and middle left: A series of dynamic layers creates a long season of interest. In spring geums, Lychnis flos-cuculi 'White Robin' and Iris sibirica cultivars are prominent among the foliage foil of the later layers.

Middle centre, middle right, and bottom left: in midsummer the purples of Astilbe chinensis var. taquetii 'Purpurlanze' and Lythrum salicaria 'Zigeunerblut' take over the display.

Bottom centre and right: In late summer and autumn the purples fade to be replaced by the yellows of Rudbeckia fulgida var. deamii and crocosmias.

Opposite: In late summer devil's bit scabious, Succisa pratensis, spills onto the path, adding to the multi-sensory, immersive experience as people swish through the flowers.

John Lewis Rain Garden
Design: Nigel Dunnett
Implementation: 2015

The John Lewis rain garden is Central London's first streetside rain garden. It is located on Victoria Street, at the head offices of the John Lewis Group, just around the corner from Victoria Station. The site is immediately outside the main entrance to the building, on the street and pavement, and adjacent to the portico that provides a dry drop-off point for visitors. Previously the site was completely paved and cobbled, apart from two poorly shaped trees. Indeed, the whole immediate area is devoid of trees and green space. This lack of green, combined with the flood-prone nature of Victoria, made the John Lewis site the prime choice for the creation of a new rain garden. It was funded by the Victoria Business Improvement District (Victoria BID) as part of their Green Infrastructure Audit process, whereby suitable sites for retro-fitting green features that promote biodiversity, flood prevention and human enjoyment are identified and supported.

The John Lewis rain garden is a prime example of turning 'grey to green' and of retrofitting green infrastructure. It also contains several examples of a climate-change adapted landscape: the rain garden itself; a storm-water planter; and minimal irrigation urban planters. It is a landscape adapted for both extreme rainfall events and droughts.

The main area of the rain garden is planted with a naturalistic mix of grasses and perennials to deliver a low-maintenance, beautiful and long-season visual effect.

Promoting biodiversity is a key objective, and there is a wealth of flowering plants to support pollinating insects in this predominantly 'grey' part of the city. The rain garden is sited in a typical urban canyon – windy and exposed – and plants must be hardy in these conditions. Although they need to cope with periodic wet conditions, in a street-side location in Central London there are also likely to be prolonged dry and potentially very hot conditions. It is important to emphasize that in such locations, a rain garden is not a 'wetland'. The chosen species are therefore tolerant of a wide range of environmental conditions. Some native British species have been used, but there are also a wide range of plants from elsewhere.

It was extremely important to the building users that the rain garden should present a clean and tidy image that looks effective throughout the year, as befits the head offices of a major company. Therefore, there is a solid and regular structure of evergreen hedges (*Sarcococca confusa*), which is highly scented when flowering in the winter and early spring) within the garden to provide a sense of order and formality among the naturalistic planting. The plants are established within a silver-grey granite gravel mulch that matches the colour of the building. The mulch creates a clean and neat surface that looks effective in the winter, although the intention is that during the growing season, the vegetation covers the mulch completely. The mulch also acts as a weed control, and creates a stable surface should the rain garden fill with water.

Left: The potential for the environmental agenda to drive the installation of diverse urban plantings as part of 'Green Infrastructure' is immense. There would be very little incentive to undertake this dramatic transformation of sterile and sealed hard surface to a plant-rich landscape if it were purely for decorative reasons. However, the opportunity to use the landscape to meet a real environmental challenge (localized flooding) provided the catalyst for the installation of new planting that helps with that problem, but which also looks good, and is a valuable resource for pollinating insects.

Top left: Previously the site consisted of a hard, impervious surface with two over-mature and misshapen trees.
Top right: Setting out the new plantings, with naturalistic perennial and grass mixes, and linear hedges of sweet box to add a sense of order and formality in this highly urban context.

Centre left: Rainwater from the downpipes from the roof (which run down inside the portico columns) is diverted first into a raised stormwater planter and then as overspill into the rain garden.
Centre right: The gravel mulch aids water infiltration, creates a neat appearance, and acts as a weed control layer as seen here in late spring.
Bottom row: The plants start to establish and have filled out by the time this picture (right) was taken in late summer.

London Wetland Centre Rain Garden
Design: Nigel Dunnett
Implementation: 2010

This was my first rain garden project and it set out to show, in a stylized way, how the whole system works, connecting a house or buildings with the garden or surrounding landscape. A converted shipping container supports a green roof – the first absorption point for rainfall hitting the building. Any excess water drains off the roof into a water cistern via a rain chain. That can then overflow into a series of rain garden features, each of which overflows into the next. As it does so, the water becomes increasingly clean – the sequence includes an ornamental reed bed water treatment area.

Below: A circular level boardwalk constructed using durable deckboards made from recycled plastic, provides access to all parts of the garden. In the wetter areas of the garden, primulas such as *P. florindae* are planted along with native wetland species such as purple loosetrife, *Lythrum salicaria*. The wetland character is maintained in the dryer parts of the site too, with the upright *Calamagrostis x acutiflora* 'Karl Foerster' creating a reedbed-like feel. While most of the rain garden features are unlined to let water infiltrate back into the soil, the lowest one in the chain is lined and planted with variegated reeds, *Phragmites communis* 'Variegata' as a water filtration bed – water exits this bed into a stream that flows though the garden. Tall 'Creature Towers' provide a permanent sculptural element. These are vertical structures of stacked waste materials and wild bee habitat panels, along with a bird feeding table and nest box – they were constructed by volunteers, using left-over and waste materials found on the wider site.

Top left: Lush planting with the white-flowered British native of wet meadows, meadowsweet (*Filipendula ulmaria*) flowering with the golden yellow Central European species of damp places, giant fleabane (*Inula magnifica*).

Top right and centre left: A stepping stone path over the stream creates an exciting experience and gives the impression of going over deep water. In reality the water is only a few centimetres deep over a concrete platform with the stream running through a large pipe beneath. The water level rises and falls depending on rainfall.

Bottom left: The seedheads of *Rodgersia pinnata* 'Superba' on the left in the first of the rain gardens in the sequence, with the variegated reeds further along the chain.

Right: A central path to the garden pavilion, created from a converted shipping container with a habitat green roof, has a 'dry stream' running alongside it. This can fill with water runoff from the roof of the pavilion, but is a play feature with boulders for most of the time when it is dry. On the side of the pavilion is a 'periscope' that gives a view onto the roof from ground level.

Sheffield Grey to Green Project

Design: Nigel Dunnett and Sheffield City Council
Implementation: 2016

At the time of writing, the Grey to Green scheme in Sheffield was the UK's largest urban water-sensitive design project, and a radical one at that. It involved converting an inner city four-lane highway into a two-lane road taking mainly public transport, then making the liberated space into a linear series of rain gardens and bioswales. Interestingly, one of the main objectives of the large areas of new planting was to create a very attractive setting for new inward investment and economic activity in this part of the city. The planting is highly dynamic and naturalistic, and has a relatively high proportion of evergreen species to maintain winter interest.

As I've noted already, high quality horticulture and exciting complex planting design is usually the missing link in urban water-sensitive schemes. This is so surprising, given that it is the combination of soils and vegetation that makes it all work, and it's the planted element that's by far the most visible. We set out to create a scheme that featured diverse plantings that were completely different in character and content to standard landscape planting.

The plant mixtures contain plants with a wide range of ecological tolerances from those that prefer wetter conditions to those that are happy when it's very dry. The scheme is therefore very resliient to changes in weather from month to month and season to season.

The scheme was set out according to the the random planting method (see page 63). However, a further layer of 'order' was imposed on top of this, with linear meandering swathes of *Calamagrostis* x *acutiflora* 'Karl Foerster' which remain bolt upright through the winter.

I was curious to know whether people on the street would welcome this very natural scheme in a highly urban and unexpected setting – it is totally different to the usual sort of low-diversity and uniform public planting they would be familiar with. I had some students carry out hundreds of interviews with passers-by and the response was overwhelmingly positive, with more than 80 per cent of respondents thinking it was very suited to the surroundings – in fact about 60 of the 350 people interviewed had actually changed their daily route so that they could experience these plantings. It has provided very strong evidence to me of the need to create truly 'green streets'.

Below: Concept visual that shows the function of the rain garden and bioswale in capturing, storing, cleaning and infiltrating the surface water runoff from the road and pavements.

Top left: The stormwater bioswales in construction.

Top right: The bioswales in late summer, with yellow *Rudbeckia fulgida* var. *deamii*, white *Gaura lindheimeri* and *Kniphiofia triangularis*. Stormwater runoff can flow into the swales along the whole length of the road.

Bottom left: Pink sea thrift, *Armeria maritima*, along the drier edges of the swales.

Bottom right: Rain garden features offer such exciting planting design possibilities and it's essential that they look very attractive in visible locations, for their continued success and acceptance. Here, *Iris sibirica* 'Tropic Night' flowers among the foliage of rushes, *Juncus effusus*, and tufted hair grass, *Deschampsia cespitosa*.

Overleaf: Big clumps of *Eupatorium cannabinum* 'Flore Pleno' in late summer among the seedheads of *Deschampsia cespitosa*, and the upright *Calamagrostis* x *acutiflora* 'Karl Foerster' behind. It's difficult to believe that this is an inner city streetscape.

DRY PLANTING: ROOF GARDENS, GREEN ROOFS AND PODIUMS

While water-sensitive design addresses too much rainwater, equally it must deal with too little. Ironically, many sites might have to deal with both situations in any given year. There's a strong moral case for not creating plantings that are dependent on watering for their long-term survival if that water is treated drinking water, as is often the case. Of course, there's less of a problem if the water used is harvested rainwater, but what happens in an excessively dry year? There's a lot of sense in making plantings, gardens and landscapes that do not need so much of it in the first place. Also, with water use restrictions becoming increasing likely in the future, it just won't be possible to rely on having endless water at our disposal for keeping water-thirsty gardens looking green.

I regularly work with 'dry' plantings; they're my staple for urban applications. My main inspiration is the 'steppes' – vegetation adapted to continental climates with hot dry summers and cold winters. Steppes are grasslands and meadows, and I have an affinity for their looseness and movement. Where soils are a bit deeper, shrubs can establish, but the environment is too hostile for large trees. I've used this reference landscape as the model for the plantings at the Barbican, London. However, depending on where you are in the world, there is much to work with as your starting point, whether it be desert or Mediterranean vegetations, for example.

This type of planting is particularly suited to roof garden applications because only a certain depth of soil or growing medium is possible in these situations, and therefore the areas are very prone to drying out. Couple this with increased wind and sun exposure in many cases, and they can be very stressful indeed. In fact, 'extensive' green roofs (those with very thin depths of substrate or growing medium) mostly use the 'durable' type of plants.

Above: Although green roofs are usually thought of as dry features, they work well in a tropical climate as shown by this green roof in Singapore.

Left: This roof garden in Melbourne, Australia, has plenty of opportunities for the use of climbing plants and vines, as well as for plants on the ground.

Opposite: In dense urban areas, rooftops present huge opportunities for increasing biodiversity and habitat, including the creation of sky-rise wetlands and water bodies.

Moorgate Crofts, Rotherham

Design: Nigel Dunnett and Rotherham Borough Council
Implementation: 2004

This was my first proper roof terrace planting, and the plant choices arose directly out of extensive trials on drought-tolerant roof garden planting at the University of Sheffield. The building is a business start-up centre, with an accessible and visible roof terrace. At the time (and still now) the range of plants typically used in green roofs and roof gardens was very limited, or the roof gardens required a lot of irrigation to keep them lush and green. The plantings at Moorgate Crofts aimed to create visual interest throughout the year, with a mulch of stone aggregate for a neat winter appearance. All the plants came from steppe and dry meadow habitats (with the exception of kniphofias, which my research has shown to be remarkably resilient in this situation).

The growing medium is 100–200mm (4–8in) deep across the surface, and there is no irrigation. Maintenance consists simply of an annual cut back in late winter, with all cuttings removed. Over time, the plantings have evolved into the most incredible flowering steppe grassland, with breathtaking displays of pasque flowers (*Pulsatilla vulgaris*) and cowslips (*Primula veris*) in the spring. I've monitored these plantings every year since establishment, and they directly informed the much more extensive rooftop plantings at the Barbican.

Opposite: The 'steppe' type of dry meadow planting requires no irrigation. Here *Sisyrinchium striatum* and the purple flowers of chives, *Allium schoenoprasum* are prominent with the grey foliage of *Stachys byzantina*.
Top left: the drought-tolerant blue oat grass, *Helicotrichon sempervirens*, with the self-seeding 'pop-up' pink flowers of *Erodium manascavii*.
Top right: Cowslip, *Primula veris*, in spring.
Centre left: In early summer, the yellow flowers of *Euphorbia cyparissias* create a carpet with the seedheads of pasque flowers, *Pulsatilla vulgaris*, above.
Centre right: Pulsatillas in full flower in April.
Bottom left: The beautiful purple flowers and stems of the grass *Festuca amethystina*, with sea campion, *Silene uniflora*.
Bottom right: in autumn seed heads dominate, here with late-flowering asters.

Future Nature

Sharrow School, Sheffield
Design: Nigel Dunnett and Sheffield City Council
Implementation: 2006

I took a completely different approach with the roof-garden plantings at Sharrow School. The intention here was to create a structured urban wilderness that would be a haven for birds and insects, but would also capture the imagination of children at the school because of its colour and visual spectacle. I used a wide range of techniques to create the garden, including direct sowing of annual and perennial meadows (which were not restricted to native species alone); planting of perennials at low density and seeding around them; laying some pregrown green roof turf to my specification; and also keeping some areas free for natural colonization. These quickly became filled with beautiful urban pop-up plants such as verbascums, purple toadflax (*Linaria purpurea*) and wall valerian (*Centranthus ruber*).

Below: A beautiful dry meadow mix in early summer with the purple flowers of chives, *Allium schoenoprasum* and orange flowers of fox and cubs, *Hieracium aurantiacum*.

Opposite top left: The completed school with its designed 'urban wilderness' on top.

Opposite top right: Yellow flowers of the drought-tolerant *Anthemis tinctorial*

Opposite middle left: A mass of chives in late spring: these will grow in wet conditions as well as dry.

Opposite bottom: Some parts of the roof were left along to encourage spontaneous colonization of urban species such as purple toadflax, *Linaria purpurea* (left) while in other areas (right) vegetation such as this Pictorial Meadow seed mix, featuring the annual *Silene armeria*, has been introduced.

Garden of Pooled Talents, University of Sheffield Campus

Design: Nigel Dunnett and Broadbent Studio
Implementation: 2016

It's important to emphasize that although we're mostly talking about roof gardens in this section, all the principles work equally well in dry places on the ground – there is such great potential to fill dry areas with exciting roof garden planting that doesn't need to be watered! The Garden of Pooled Talents is such as example. Underneath is a concrete deck – it's a podium (elevated) landscape even though it's on the ground, a very common occurrence in cities. We were able to mound up the growing medium to create a rippling landform. A typical green roof growing medium was used – 70 per cent crushed brick and expanded clay granules (tall aggregate to maximize drainage), 20 per cent green waste compost (for moisture retention) and 10 per cent silt (to give the growing medium some structure). No irrigation is given.

Below: The garden contains large galvanized metal sculptures in the shape of giant spoons that symbolize the creative mixing of disciplines in a university environment. In late summer, *Kniphofia* 'Green Jade' flowers with the blue of *Aster* x *frikartii* 'Mönch' and *Perovskia* 'Blue Spire'.

Above left: The flowers of the blue oat grass, *Helicotrichon sempervirens*. Although on the ground, this uses all the techniques of green roof design to create diverse, no-irrigation landscapes.

Top right: Later summer seed heads among the bright crimson flowers of the steppe plant *Dianthus carthusianorum*.

Bottom: Where soils are deeper, taller structural plants are used. Here the upright grass *Calamagrostis* x *acutiflora* 'Overdam' is used with white *Aquilegia vulgaris* 'Nivea' in a slighty more shady part of the garden.

CASE STUDY: THE BARBICAN BEECH GARDENS

Design: Nigel Dunnett
Implementation: Spring 2015
Client: The City of London Corporation and The Barbican Estate Office

The Barbican is Europe's largest cultural, arts and conference venue, and a residential estate housing 4000 people. It's a world-renowned icon of Brutalist architecture, built mainly in the 1970s as a utopian vision of a new urban village, with shops and top-quality cultural facilities on the doorstep of residents in the heart of London, and all vehicles, roads and car parks underground, so that at the surface, all the open spaces, plazas and gardens are completely for people to enjoy without motor traffic of any sort. Like many open spaces in high-density urban development, the gardens, courtyards and water bodies at the Barbican are actually roof gardens, 'podium landscapes', and 'landscapes above structure', even though they may appear to be firmly rooted on the ground. A requirement to rewaterproof part of the Barbican podium in 2015 presented an exciting opportunity to completely rethink what a roof garden could be, and to explore how these spaces could be made more sustainable and ecologically valuable.

The previous plantings were very traditional in nature, consisting of large trees, shrubs, lawns and seasonal bedding plants. Although green and lush, this was sustained through an automatic irrigation system, using drinkable mains water. A key consideration for the new scheme was that the City of London Corporation, the local authority that manages the spaces, no longer wished to rely on such irrigation systems, partly because of the potential for water-use restrictions and shortages in Central London as a result of future droughts. This is therefore a pioneering example of a climate change-adapted landscape.

Opposite: In spring, the rounded mounds of the short cultivar *Euphorbia characias* 'Humpty Dumpty' stand out among the cut-back grasses and perennials. A spring layer of red *Tulipa praestans* 'Fusilier' stands out strongly against the green.

Top: The 'power of three' rule was applied in selecting plants for the mixes, so that at any one time two or three plant species are making the visual display over the entire area. This is a multi-layered planting – here multi-stem *Amelanchier lamarckii* and *Prunus* 'Sunset Boulevard' are flowering above the herbaceous layer.

Above: There's a strong, complementary synergy between the naturalistic plantings and the strongly architectural and urban framework.

Because of the radical change in landscape character that was involved, we undertook a lot of public and resident consultation over these changes. Three main issues emerged repeatedly: concern over removal of existing large trees; attachment to the annual seasonal bedding displays; and worries over a dead-looking winter appearance of perennial-based plantings. At first these seemed to be insurmountable challenges: loading requirements meant that we could not replace the existing large trees, and the use of intensive seasonal annual displays went against the whole ethos of the new scheme.

However, further discussions revealed that a large part of the attachment to the trees was that they supported birds. Seeing and hearing birds was a joy for residents and I was able to say that the new plantings would have great wildlife value – supporting invertebrates and pollinating insects to a far great degree than previously. In fact nesting birds have now returned into the gardens too. Discussion also revealed that support for annual bedding displays was related to a love of bright colour in the urban surroundings, and I was able to say that the new scheme would be even more colourful over a larger area. Finally, the negative perceptions of perennial plantings being rather dull and dead-looking in winter prompted me to include a large proportion of evergreen grasses and perennials which have now come to define the character of the Barbican plantings throughout the year.

In all of these ways, and more, the consultations taught me a valuable lesson: to get to the real issues behind points that are being raised, rather than taking everything at face value. There is no doubt that resident's concerns over the winter appearance resulted in a greatly improved final scheme, and changed the way I have worked from then on.

Moving from a traditional municipal landscape with simple planting of groundcover species in large monocultural blocks, rigorous cultivation of bare soil between plants and neatly trimmed lawns to a highly naturalistic scheme with no lawns, very diverse plantings, no desire for bare soil and an encouraging of a dynamic, self-sustaining character was hugely challenging for all concerned. An analysis of sun, shade and shadow was the starting point for the design, and this resulted in three main planting zones: open, sunny and exposed; areas receiving shade at some point in the day; and mainly shaded areas. The possible depth of growing medium was also a determining factor. Most of the site would support a maximum depth of 300–350mm (12–14in), suitable for perennials and grasses, but some enabled greater depths for trees and shrubs. A typical free-draining green roof substrate was the planting medium.

Below: A section showing a typical 'build-up' of the green roof system at the Barbican. There's a base layer of very infertile, aggregate-based growing medium with little or no organic matter (less than 10%). An upper layer of a substrate with slightly more organic matter (20%) to support greater plant growth. Where trees were possible because of underlying structural support, growing medium depths could be up to 900mm (35.5in) in depth, but typically the depth is 200-300mm (8-12in).

Right: A microclimate analysis, together with growing medium depth (both of which are related to moisture availability), drove the plant selection for the scheme. Red = total shade all day; blue = shade for most of the day; dark purple = half light/half shade; light purple = full sun all day.

Below. The schematic planting plan for Beech Gardens at the Barbican. The scheme consisted of four different plant mixes according to growing medium depth and sun/shade. Trees and shrubs are located individually (situated formally in lines and a grid that reflects underlying building structural support columns). A further layer added structural 'order' within the loose naturalistic plantings. This consists of monocultural blocks of structural perennials and grasses.

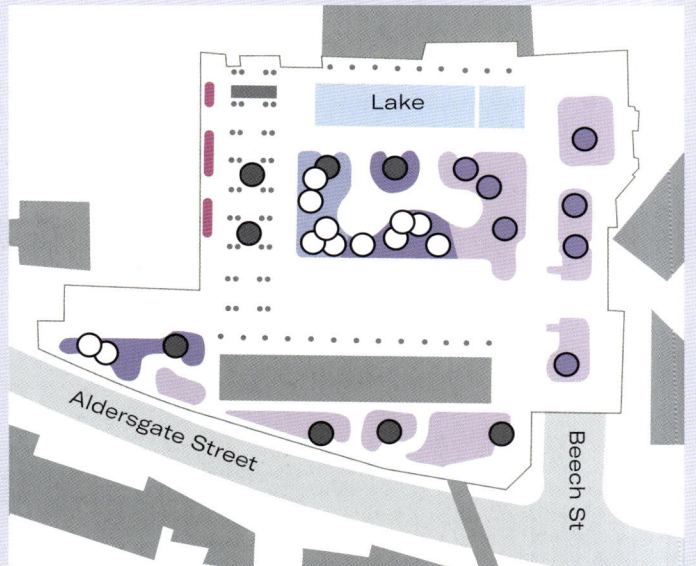

 Small multi-stem tree: *Betula utilis* var. *jacquemontii* & *Prunus* 'Sunset Boulevard'

 Amelanchier lamarckii (multi-stem)

 Libertia formosa (group of 7)

 Phlomis russeliana (group of 7)

 Miscanthus sinensis 'Undine' (group of 3)

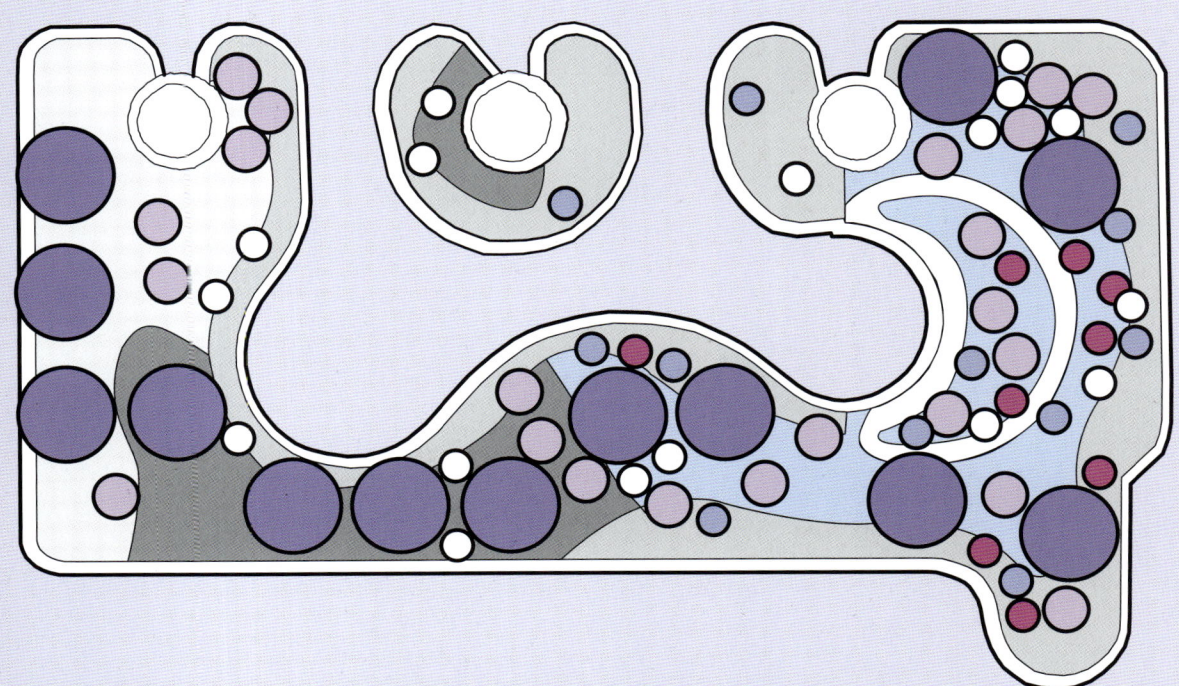

Future Nature

Top left: Two different mixes were used in this bed at the Barbican, and the boundary between the two was marked out in spray paint. Multi-stem birches are placed first.

Top right: The first anchor species are placed. Here it is a matrix species: the grass *Sesleria nitida*. It's also a 'cross-over' species in that is occurs in both the mixes. I set out plantings one species at a time across a whole area, so that I could clearly see the patterns. This setting out follows the COG principle where there is typically a group of three individuals and an outlier of one.

Middle left: In another planting bed, there is the matrix anchor of the grass *Sesleria nitida* and a framework anchor of *Euphorbia characias* subsp. *wulfenii*.

Middle right: Additional satellite species are gradually added around these anchors, species by species, building up groupings using the COG principle. Remaining spaces are filled by free floaters until all the gaps are filled.

Bottom left: A completed area, with the plants in the ground.

Opposite: Red *Tulipa praestans* 'Fusilier' is flowering among the lime-green flowers of *Euphorbia polychroma* and *E. characias* subsp. *wulfenii*.

The reference point for the new scheme was therefore an ecologically equivalent wild plant community: the steppe. Steppe grasslands occur naturally in continental climates with thin soils, very hot, dry summers and cold winters and contain a huge diversity of grasses, bulbs and flowering plants. At the Barbican, three main types of planting were used: a) 'steppe meadow' plantings for full sun and relatively shallow soil depths (consisting of bulbs, perennials and grasses only); b) 'shrub-steppe' plantings on relatively deeper substrate depths where woody plants could be used, but with a similar mix of perennials and grasses; and c) woodland and woodland edge in the shadier, cooler parts of the site. These shadier areas included numerous white flowers to bring light into the darker places.

The design concept was to create continuous 'waves of colour' that erupt across the site from spring until autumn as new layers continually emerge and over-top the fading earlier flowering plants, all within an evergreen matrix of grasses and structural perennials. These layers are composed of just two or three key species at any one time, repeated over the entire area to deliver large-scale drama, while the intimacy of the mixes and combinations gives visual delight at the smaller scale. It makes an ever-changing scene, all held together by a tight structural framework of anchor plants.

Maintenance consists of a series of operations to maintain high visual quality. As far as possible, seed heads and the remains of perennials are allowed to stand over the winter. However as soon as a species becomes visually untidy it is cut back wholesale across the site at any point from the summer onwards. In this way, the plantings gradually thin out over the autumn and winter and the plantings become more and more open again. These are dynamic plantings and will take on a life of their own in the medium term: self-seeding is encouraged and it is inevitable that some species will do better than others. Management is about guiding the development of the plantings in the spirit in which they were designed, and a management plan and training is essential.

Previous page: Beech Gardens in midsummer with *Achillea* 'Terracotta', white *Lychnis coronaria* 'Alba', purple *Salvia nemorosa* 'Caradonna' and taller red *Croscosmia* 'Lucifer'.

Below: The flowering year starts out with an intricate spring layer of bulbs (*Tulipa turkestanica* and *Tulipa praestans*) and low-growing dry meadow and steppe perennials such as *Primula veris* and *Pulsatilla vulgaris*.

Overall, the new scheme has resulted in a 70 per cent reduction in water use – some handwatering is possible in very dry periods. There has been no increase in the total amount of maintenance time required, despite the fact that these are vastly more complex plantings compared to what went before. A new gardening group of about 20 residents work alongside the main gardeners every Friday morning to help with routine maintenance, but also to do some of the more detailed elements of 'garden craft' that is not possible with the main garden teams. This might involve, for example, transplanting seedlings of self-sowers, or detailed weeding where this might be necessary. Getting communities involved in looking after their community spaces is often held up as an aspiration, but it can be very difficult to achieve. At the Barbican, the dramatic and colourful nature of the plantings has helped to pull people into wishing to be involved in their care. And a very noticeable change is that previously, many people visited the Barbican to photograph the architecture but never the gardens. Now people visit to take photos purely of the gardens!

Top left: Drifts of *Salvia nemorosa* 'Caradonna' with *Phlomis* and *Euphorbia wulfenii*
Top middle: Alliums flowering amongst the steppe grasses (*Sesleria nitida* and *Helicotrichon sempervirens*) with crimson *Knautia macedonica*.
Top right: The same plantings later in the summer when seed heads play an important role.

Centre left: This is a climate-adapted, resilient planting. At the end of a dry summer without automatic irrigation, the grey and blue foliage of the drought-tolerant plants really stands out, here with the steely blue flowers of *Echinops ritro* 'Veitch's Blue' and the softer blue of Russian sage, *Perovskia atriplicifolia*.
Centre middle: *Aster amellus* in late summer in the steppe meadow.
Centre right: The combination of white amelanchier blossom in spring with the vivid bracts of *Euphorbia wulfenii* is a real signature planting at the Barbican

Bottom left: High summer, with *Kniphofia* 'Tawny King' and *Achillea* 'Terracotta'.
Bottom middle: Late summer with *Oreganum laevigatum* 'Herrenhausen'
Bottom right: In autumn and through the winter, monocultural groups of *Miscanthus sinensis* 'Undine' give order and structure to the looser naturalistic plantings, and make a dramatic contrast with the evergreen rounded euphorbias.

Above: The Barbican is a prime example of uncompromising Brutalist architecture. The naturalistic planting works in strong synergy with the architectural context – in fact both are enhanced – the architecture benefits from the naturalness of the planting, which itself is enhanced by the hardness of the context. A very common comment from visitors is that it is 'like being in the middle of a wildflower meadow in the middle of the city'.

Right: The plant mixes included a proportion of short-lived but quick flowering or self-seeding plants to give initial impact, but which over the years would become less prominent as plantings matured and closed up available gaps for seed regeneration.

Above: The plantings are based on successive eruptions or 'waves of colour' over the course of a year. Here, *Salvia nemorosa* 'Caradonna' and purple alliums burst through the grassy matrix, with drifts of pale yellow *Sisyrinchium striatum*. The vivid red splashes of *Papaver orientale* 'Goliath' energize the whole scheme. Pathways between the planting beds and places to sit create a real immersive experience for people.

THE WEB OF LIFE

So far, we've been focusing solely on plants and planting. But, of course, vegetation provides food sources for other life in the garden, whether this be nectar, pollen, seeds or foliage. Therefore an important element of 'Future Nature' concerns how we provide for wider biodiversity, or the 'web of life'. Where possible I like to integrate artful habitat structures into plantings so that as well as the direct food sources there is also shelter, particularly for invertebrates. It's something I saw done extensively in nature gardens in Holland in the 1990s, and I was determined to develop my own versions. What particularly struck me about these Dutch examples, compared to the little bee and bug hotel structures that I came across in the UK, was their sheer scale. They were sculptures in their own right. It made me think that if you were going to integrate artwork and sculpture into a garden or a planting, then why not, in the spirit of everything else here, make it multi-functional.

My own garden

In my garden, which is steeply sloping, I've divided the plantings into separate sections using 'wave-form' log piles. They give an essential element of order. Unlike normal terrace walls, which tend to go along the contour lines to create flatter areas for planting or for use, the log pile walls go against the contours and flow up and down the slopes. In this sense they replicate the pattern of the dry-stone walls that divide the fields all around me, which have a similarly curved rather than flat profile. Of course, the log sections gradually rot away and the walls subside. You could see that as part of the process, and artful in itself. But I like to keep the integrity of the shapes, so each winter I top them up to keep the same wave-form pattern. As well as providing plenty of habitat opportunities for invertebrates, the log piles gradually become naturalized with ferns and self-seeding plants such as foxgloves (*Digitalis purpurea*). They also develop a whole new 'flora' of fungi that sprout out like flowers from the logs in the autumn.

Opposite top: The log piles become submerged and mostly hidden by the growth of the surrounding planting by the end of summer.
Opposite bottom: The log piles in early spring, with the surrounding perennials and grasses cut back to ground level. Each year there is some decay and so an annual task is to refresh the top of the piles with new logs to retain the shapes. The mix of old and new is attractive in itself.

Top left: Spring is marked by the fresh green emerging foliage of perennials and grasses and the upright spikes of foxglove, *Digitalis purpurea*.
Top right: The energy of summer with *Campanula lactiflora* 'Loddon Anna', *Thalictrum* 'Elin' behind, the bracts of *Euphorbia wulfenii*, and the flowers of the grass *Deschampsia cespitosa*.

Bottom left: In October the seedheads of *Deschampsia cespitosa* mix with the flowers and seed heads of *Rudbeckia fulgida* var *deamii*.
Bottom right: A dusting of snow in winter.

Overleaf: There are five different wave-form piles here, one behind the other. Passing by you experience a fascinating and changing interplay of shapes.

Opposite: The author's Chelsea Flower Show Garden in 2018, sponsored by the Royal Horticultural Society (RHS), featured diverse multi-layered plantings and vertical 'creature towers', consisting of a series of layers fixed to an upright post, each filled with materials to encourage their use by a wide range of invertebrates.

Above: The author's Show Garden for the 2016 RHS Hampton Court Flower Show again featured 'creature towers', here with a bird nesting box. The holes drilled in wood are perfect places for use by solitary (non-hive) bees, which are excellent pollinators. The surrounding plants support those very same pollinators.

Right: The author's Chelsea Flower Show Garden in 2013 with a pavilion that supports a 'biodiverse' green roof and a rain chain that channels rainwater runoff into a rain garden below. On the pavilion is the 'tree of life' artwork that is composed of circular 'habitat panels' filled with nesting and sheltering opportunities for invertebrates.

Future Nature

CULTIVATION GUIDELINES

The approach to planting design described in this book opens itself out to endless experimentation. That's part of the fun – there are no ideal plant combinations. In fact, it could be argued that a certain formulaic approach to naturalistic planting has developed over the past decades, with the same plants used in the same sort of combinations, and most specialist plant nurseries offering similar ranges. The relatively new 'random planting' approach has a tendency to take this even further, by offering recipes and standardized plant or seed mixtures that can be used wherever suitable site conditions can be found. This might be all right as a basic starting point, but the most interesting things happen when you start to deviate from the formula and try out your own thing.

Similarly, it's difficult to be prescriptive about all the different establishment and management techniques that could be used. In this final section, we'll take a look at a few standard prescriptions that I use most of the time, but remember – these are here to be played around with and altered!

SITE PREPARATION

Everything starts from the site conditions that provide the basis for deciding which plants you will select. Generally, it won't work the other way around – drastic alterations and modifications to the site in order to suit some predetermined set of plants that you are insisting on growing.

I rarely, if ever, follow the traditional horticultural practice of bumping up the fertility of the soil to grow stupendous specimens of plants. As we saw earlier in the book, this will only encourage aggressive 'dominator' plants. Instead, I prefer to work with moderately stressful conditions. I encourage free drainage, however, and loosen up heavily compacted sites.

The absolute key consideration is working with weed-free conditions at the outset. Unless you have significant weeding resources available to you, then you will want to ensure that the site is as clean as possible before you introduce your vegetation. Depending on your philosophy and preferred methods, you will either do this organically or chemically.

Sterile mulches

Once you have done as much as possible to ensure that the site is clean, there is an organic (non-chemical) approach that will help you establish your required planting with minimum competition from weeds. This is the use of *sterile, weed-free soil mulches*. By spreading a mulch of a weed-free material over the top of the existing surface you will be able to establish your plants into a clean environment; they will be able to get their roots down into the soil beneath but weed seeds or vegetative fragments in that soil will be prevented from pushing up through the mulch. Sand, gravels and weed-free green-waste compost will fit the bill for this and will contribute no additional fertility to the site. Indeed these materials have low fertility and will result in tight, tough plants, albeit smaller than individuals of the same species that you might be familiar with from flower border conditions.

For this to be effective, mulch depths need to be a minimum of 100mm (4in) and up to 200mm (8in). Using artificial green roof substrates for planting gives the same effect. The use of these materials might seem a significant up-front cost, but they will save significant amounts of time in terms of long-term maintenance.

Above: A 200mm (8in) layer of weed-free municipal green-waste compost is spread over nutrient-poor subsoil at Trentham, prior to the planting of the perennial meadow areas. The mulch provides a non-competitive start for the newly established planting.

Opposite top: Peter Korn uses a deep mulch of coarse sand (often spread directly over lawn grass as a means of establishing new plantings from scratch) as a completely weed-free and hard-growing environment for plantings. It's a very effective method, but the addition of slow-release fertilizer is advised otherwise plant growth can be very slow. Photo taken in Peter Korn's garden.

Opposite middle: Planting into gravel or similar aggregate is another effective method of promoting hardy growth. Here, drought-tolerant plants such as yuccas and *Stachys byzantina* are established in a 100mm (4in) layer of aggregate.

This page: Plants were established with a 100mm (4in) aggregate mulch in both the Sheffield Grey to Green scheme (above) and the John Lewis Rain Garden (right) to create a free-draining, weed-free surface, which is also clean and crisp in the winter before the vegetation was fully established.

Cultivation Guidelines

PLANTING AND SEEDING

Establishment from planting
When planting, I typically work at a density of 9–16 plants per square metre (1¼sq yd). This might seem high, but remember that this is not conventional border planting with overfed and watered plants. If you think of the density of plants in a meadow then this is actually very low! The aim is for the vegetation to close up in its first year, reducing the need for any weeding into the future. Despite the general no or low irrigation rule, it's important to make sure plants are well-established and therefore if the weather is very dry for the first 4–6 weeks or so, regular watering is essential.

Above: A yellow-themed perennial seed mix interacts with a red-pink-purple mix, and streaks of blue and pink intersect other perennial mixes. Working with colour-themed mixes in this way is similar to the brush strokes of painting. Seed mix design: Nigel Dunnett

Top right: Alternating bands of different colour-themed perennial meadow mixes, created from seed, line this path in the London Olympic Park. Yellow *Anthemis tinctoria* is prominent, along with purple *Centaurea scabiosa*. Seed mix design: Nigel Dunnett

Opposite top: The setting-out density of plants at the Beech Gardens, Barbican. This mix includes shorter-lived 'pop-up' plants for visual effect in the first one or two years, as well as more durable, longer-term plants.

Opposite bottom: A similar plant density for the planted meadow at Trentham. Although the density of plants might seem high, compared to the number of plants per square metre that would be the outcome of seeding, this is a relatively low density of plants. In both these examples, working with lower-fertility soils or growing media was essential.

Seeding
Seeding is one of the hallmarks of the Sheffield School. It allows large areas to be filled with naturalistic planting in a way that would be hugely expensive if using plants alone. It's been a mainstay for me, especially using 'pop-up' plants. A clean, cultivated seed bed is essential. Some books refer to the possibility of being able to over-sow existing grasslands or lawns by very roughly raking them over or otherwise disturbing them first to open up some ground for the seedlings to establish into. But really, this is a waste of time because nine times out of ten the seedlings will just be out-competed by the existing grasses.

Very detailed information about making up perennial meadow seed mixes is given in my colleague James Hitchmough's book *Sowing Beauty* and I will not repeat any of that information here. However, I rarely use perennial seed mixes on their own in visible, usable, or high-profile locations. This is because perennials tend to take two years from seed before they get to meaningful flowering size. In the meantime their appearance is little different to a mass of weeds coming up on a neglected site. It is also inherently highly risky because of potential failure of the seeding, and a real lack of predictability about which seeds will be successful – the balance of plants in a mix can't be guaranteed.

However, for annuals the situation is different. They will flower within a few months of sowing, weeds will not be noticeable, and each year there is the chance to clean the site and start again. The ideal combination is to include some annuals within a perennial mix for some visual interest in year one. Typically I include around 10 per cent of annuals in a perennial seed mix, and use what I call 'slender annuals' such as cornflowers, flaxes and coreopsis – plants that go straight up without making big foliage rosettes or canopies that will eliminate the establishing perennials. In experimental work that I've done, I've found that putting this proportion of annuals in a mix actually reduces weed invasion because it closes up all potential gaps where weeds can get in.

Above: These perennial meadows in the London Queen Elizabeth Olympic Park were created using native UK species, but with a very low percentage presence of grasses to maximize floral impact. Seed mix design: James Hitchmough

Right: Clump-forming grasses maintain their integrity in a perennial seed mix and create visual interest when flowering is over. Here, sheep's fescue, *Festuca ovina* is scattered through one of the Fantasticology seed mixes, with *Achillea millefolium*, and provides visual interest at the end of the season. Seed mix design: Nigel Dunnett

Top: To establish this number of plants in an area by planting rather than seeding would be much more expensive.

Bottom left: A clean seed bed with a well-worked 'tilth' of fine crumbs at the surface is essential for successful establishment. This bank is ready for sowing, in the London Olympic Park in spring 2012.

Bottom right: The same view, six months later, with an annual 'Olympic Gold' mix in full flower. Seed mix design Nigel Dunnett

Above: Being creative with meadows: here on Sheffield's ring road, some annual poppies have been mixed with a perennial wildflower meadow seed mix to give first-year colour. Naturalized alliums and cammassias give a flowering display before the main perennials take over. All were established at the same time in the autumn before this photo was taken.

Right: Where the soil is very weedy, the use of a sterile surface mulch, such as coarse sand, enables establishment of plants from a seed mix, while preventing regrowth of weed seedlings from below (the established seeds from the mix can get their roots into the soil below the mulch). Here a sowing mulch is spread over an existing weedy soil.

Top left: Seeding can also be combined with planting. In this example, perennials were planted into the sand mulch at low density, before the seed mix was sown around them. The whole area was covered with biodegradable hessian netting to reduce rain erosion. The seeding and planting was done in the autumn previous to this photo, which shows the planted species emerging in the spring.

Top right: One year later, and the hessian netting has rotted away, although some sand is still visible. The purple shoots are the emerging foliage of purple cone flower, *Echinacea purpurea*, which was established from the seed mix.

Bottom: The same area later in the summer, with blue *Aster macrophyllus* and yellow *Rudbeckia fulgida* var. *deamii* (the aster and rudbeckia were planted, the echinacea seeded). Planting and seed mix design: Nigel Dunnett

CASE STUDY: THE OLYMPIC PARK FANTASTICOLOGY AREA

Perennial seed mix design: Nigel Dunnett
Spatial design: We Made That & LDA Design
Implementation: Spring 2013

The Fantasticology area at the London Olympic Park is a perfect example of the use of flower-rich perennial seed mixtures. During the Olympic Games this area was composed of a range of colour-themed, direct-sown annual mixes which I developed specifically for the park, but after the Games ended it was decided to convert these to colour-themed perennial mixes. Over the whole of the Olympic Park we were lucky to work with cleaned-up soils because of the previous contamination on site, and they were completely weed-free at the start. The perennial mixes included a proportion of the slender annuals and looked spectacular in year one, and into year two there was a good amount of reseeding. But over the next couple of years the annuals gradually died out, and now the mixes are virtually all perennial.

The Fantasticology area was created as an art installation that picked out the footprints of factories and workshops that were on the site before clearance for the making of the new park. The design of the area involved a strict pattern for the different seed mixes. What is really fascinating is that because of the annuals a complete establishment of the desired perennials was achieved, and even though the different mixes contained perennials that definitely self-seed there has been virtually no invasion of the different mixes – there are still clean boundaries between each. It's all down to getting things right at the very outset.

The seed mixes were sown at a rate of 3g (1/8oz) of seed per square metre (1¼sq yd). This is the typical sowing rate that I use, whether for perennials or annuals. In order to achieve an even distribution of seed, it is mixed with a bulking agent, spread evenly over the surface at the required amount, and then raked in.

For both perennials and annuals, I tend to use flower-rich or flower-only seed mixtures. Typical wildflower meadow mixes contain a lot of grass (80 per cent by weight of seed typically) and this can make the establishment of the perennials very problematical – which is why a lot of created meadows fail over the long term. I plant clump-forming ornamental grasses into the area, either afterwards or prior to sowing around them.

Top: A white-and-purple-themed perennial seed mix with the whites of hedge bedstraw, *Galium mollugo*, yarrow, *Achillea millefolium*, oxeye daisy, *Leucanthemum vulgare*, and purple black knapweed, *Centaurea nigra*.

Above: After five years there is still a straight-line division between these two different seed mixes. This is a direct result of achieving full vegetation cover in year one, which prevents the colonization by weeds or other plants that were not in the original seed mixes. Also key is the fact the mixes were sown onto clean, weed-free surfaces.

Top: The different colour-themed perennial seed mixes pick out the footprints of former factories and workshops on the site.
Below left: in late spring before the main flowering takes place, textural differences still mark out the different seed mixes.
Below right: Blue flax, *Linum perenne*, and red campion, *Silene dioica* alongside each other in two different perennial 'Fantasticology seed mixes.

Overleaf: The Fantasticology area in July 2018, at the height of a prolonged hot dry summer. Within this predominantly white-themed perennial meadow, with wild carrot (*Daucus carota*) in full flower, is a rectangular area of yellow perennial meadow made up of lady's bedstraw (*Galium verum*) and fernleaf yarrow (*Achillea filipendulina*) in flower.

MAKING MEADOWS

There are several ways to make meadows other than seeding. A more definite way to establish meadow vegetation is through the use of pre-grown meadow turf. This has two big advantages: it's instant and will start looking good straightaway. So long as it is weed-free in the first place, it will also largely eliminate weed invasion from the soil below. Many of the perennial Pictorial Meadow seed mixes are also available as pre-grown turf, for example. But it is the most expensive method and, as with seeding, it involves complete removal of all existing vegetation, and cultivation to make a good growing medium.

A simple and effective method is to plant perennials directly into existing lawn or grassland. Although plug plants are often recommended, these tend to be too small to establish well in competitive conditions and take some time to make any visual impact. Instead, I recommend container-grown plants, or bare root divisions, of reasonable size. Remove a section of existing grass (around 150 x 150mm/6 x 6in), excavate a planting hole, put the new plant in, and then backfill and water well. Only robust perennials will establish well in these conditions – those with leafy stems that can rise up above the grass below. The big advantage of this approach is that you can work with existing grassy areas, and that you get flowering grasses into the meadow – this matrix is part of the whole meadow experience.

Top left: One of the author's experimental areas with nursery-grown meadow turf, at Lindum Turf, North Yorkshire.

Top right: The turf is grown in thin layers of compost, over plastic sheeting to prevent rooting into the ground beneath.

Bottom left: It is amazing how much growth can be supported with this thin substrate layer, a view through the different turf meadow mixes.

Bottom right: The author's Prairie Meadow turf mix, with rudbeckias and asters visible here. The key benefit of using turf, apart from the instant effect, is that it effectively suppresses weed growth from the soil below where it is placed, representing a big maintenance advantage.

Opposite: This perennial meadow at Trentham Gardens was created using the Pictorial Meadows 'Golden Summer' perennial seed mix.

Cultivation Guidelines

Top row: The author's front garden following initial construction and installation. The lawn on the left has been newly laid with standard hard-wearing lawn turf and pictured on the right, the same lawn area after perennials have been planted into it, either as divisions from plants already in the garden, or from 2-litre pots.

Middle row: *Iris sibirica* 'Tropic Night', *Geranium sylvaticum* 'Mayflower', *Persicaria bistorta* 'Superba' and *Leucanthemum vulgare*, all naturalized into the former lawn (left). Later in the season (right), as the meadow flowers finish flowering, the naturalistic planting along the edge helps integrate the meadow into this small space.

Bottom row: Pictured left is another example in the author's garden of a former lawn converted into a long-flowering meadow. *Leucanthemum x superbum* 'Becky', *Geranium* 'Rozanne' and *Persicaria amplexicaulis* 'Rosea' are naturalized here. Pictured right is *Iris sibirica* 'White Swan' naturalized into this same area of former lawn.

Right: Here in the London Queen Elizabeth Olympic Park, the Fantasticology meadows are not cut back until late January or February. This is to allow late flowering species to perform, but as importantly, to keep the seedheads over the winter for birds. Whether a meadow area is scythed by hand, or cut with strimmers or brush cutters, or mown or flailed, it is important to remove the cuttings and compost them, so that delicate species are not smotherered and to prevent too much fertility building up in the soil.

Below: Meadows are managed by cutting off all the above-ground growth and removing it. Traditionally this will have been done from July onwards, and the material dried and used as hay for animal feed over the winter. But in a garden setting it may be advantageous to leave the cutting until the end of summer or autumn to enable later flowering species to extend the flowering display.

MAINTAINING PERENNIALS

I have a standard basic maintenance regime for the sort of naturalistic perennial plantings that this book is about. The objectives are: to minimize the amount of time-consuming input that is required; to maintain high visual quality throughout the year; to promote biodiversity and wildlife value.

Once the planting has moved beyond the establishment phase, this is my typical sequence of operations:

- By early March, all remaining dead stems and seedheads of deciduous perennials to be cut back and removed.
- Early March to mid-April: detailed weeding if required. Thin out and transplant any self-sown seedlings. Divide over-vigorous perennials. Edit the plantings if necessary. Replenish surface mulch if required – strictly to be with sterile, low fertility material such as sand, gravel, green-waste compost. Manures and fertilisers not required!
- Mid-April to mid-June: spot weeding if required. Weeding beyond this point is usually unnecessary
- Mid-June to October: minimal maintenance required. Allow the layers to build and to hide the dying-back remains of earlier flowering layers.
- October to November: remove any untidy or fallen perennial stems. The aim however is to minimize removal, and keep as many seed heads and dying-back structures in place as long as possible.

- November to February: sequential removal of dead stems and seed heads as they fall, become untidy, or detract from the visual effect. Leave all others in place. I do this systematically by cutting back and removing all of the individuals of a species that is past its best from the entire planting, and carry this out every few weeks. In this way, the winter plantings are gradually thinned, leaving only the most sturdy and robust in place until the end of the winter. The alternative is to follow standard practice and leave everything in place from October to February. This can start to look very stodgy as the winter progresses, and I prefer the gradual thinning and opening up of the plantings as the winter months go by.

Top row: Typical naturalistic perennial plantings will dry out and go brown over the winter. They should remain in good condition until early into the new year but will gradually fall over and become brittle. Pictured left is the North American garden in the London Olympic Park at the end of January. Because all the above-ground growth is dead, such plantings can be cut back to ground level in late winter and all the cuttings removed. Pictured right is the Europe garden in the Olympic Park, in early February, the area in the foreground has been cut, and the area at the back is still standing.

Bottom row: All of the cut-back growth is bagged up and taken away for disposal. However, where there are no early spring bulbs emerging beneath, it is possible also to use a rotary mower to achieve the same effect, and the very finely cut stems will form a mulch on the surface. Pictured right, the cut-back plants which will re-sprout in the spring.

Opposite top row: At the Barbican a fresh, vibrant winter look was desired for the perennial vegetation. Here maintenance has to more selective, removing deciduous perennials as they become untidy, but leaving evergreen perennials and grasses to stand. In this instance, because all the chosen plants are very robust, the plantings mostly stand uncut until spring

Opposite bottom row: In early spring in the steppe meadows, *Euphorbia characias* is flowering with the uncut clumps of the steppe grasses. Pictured right in spring, all the grasses and perennials have been cut back and the cuttings removed, apart from the evergreen euphorbia.

COPPICE MANAGEMENT

Coppicing is the cutting back to ground-level of trees and shrubs to encourage the growth of new shoots from the base. It is a traditional means of managing woodlands to produce 'small wood' for crafts and paper pulp, as opposed to the large timber from forest trees. But it is also important to note how coppice management with its alternating cycle from dark cool shade through to open warm light, as the trees are cut down and then regrow, produces a very diverse ground flora of herbaceous plants and bulbs.

Coppicing typically produces a multi-stemmed woody plant, and the new young growth can have brightly coloured stems or extra-large leaves. Some species of dogwoods (*Cornus* spp) and willows (*Salix* spp) are coppiced regularly to produce brightly coloured winter stems, for example.

Because of the association between coppicing and a diverse ground-layer of perennials, I have long felt that this is a perfect method for integrating woody plants with perennials. In the UK, we are familiar with hazel (*Corylus avellana*) or sweet chestnut (*Castanea sativa*) in our woodlands, but many, many more trees and shrubs make effective coppice plants. Moreover, some of the trees and shrubs that we consider to be difficult to control because of their suckering nature, such as sumach, *Rhus typhina*, can be effectively managed more like perennials, by periodic coppicing.

Above: Later in the year, the sumachs flame with brilliant autumn leaf colour. *Rhus typhina* and *Rhus typhina* 'Laciniata' with *Rudbeckia fulgida* var. *deamii* and golden rods (*Solidago* spp).

Left: In this combined planting by the author at RHS Harlow Carr Gardens, Yorkshire, *Rhus typhina* is planted with *Geranium psilostemon*, white *Galium mollugo*, and *Persicaria amplexicaulis*, in mixed shrubby/herbaceous plantings, maintained by coppicing. The foliage of rudbeckias is also visible.

Top left: The nut walk at Sissinghurst Castle in Kent has been hugely influential on me. Over the decades it has contained some of the most beautiful perennial shade plantings anywhere. It is, in effect, a stylized coppiced woodland of hazel (*Corylus avellana*). Here, the shuttlecock fern, *Matteuccia struthiopteris*, forms large drifts, with white bluebells, *Hyacinthoices non-scripta* 'Alba' and white trilliums.

Top right: Regularly spaced, multi-stemmed hazel stools along with the straight path bring order to the naturalistic plantings.

Bottom left: A vibrant mix of ground-covering plants, perennials, ferns, and bulbs fills the spaces in between the woody plants.

Bottom right: The Sissinghurst nut walk was a big influence on the design of the woodland garden in Sheffield Botanical Gardens. Here, sheets of native oxlip (*Primula elatior*) are planted between coppiced hazel stools. Planting Design: Nigel Dunnett

EPILOGUE

Many years ago, I was asked to give some advice to the city authorities in the Australian city of Townsville on the east coast. The climate of the region has a significant yearly dry period, so much so that locals have another name for the city: 'Brownsville', as everything dries up and ripens off. In order to counter this image, the city uses a lot of evergreen, tropical planting to liven things up, but this is hugely dependent on heavy irrigation. I went to give advice on finding native plants of the region that would look good, but which would put up with the dry conditions.

As a result, I went botanizing in the hills around the city, looking for attractive flowering plants that were still in flower despite the drought, and looking good among the dried-up savannah grasslands. I found myself delving around, taking photos of wildflowers, in a browned-off meadowy area just off the main path in a local lookout point.

Suddenly, I was approached by two women asking me what I was doing, in a way that clearly suggested I was completely and utterly crazy. I told them I was looking around for attractive plants amongst the grasses. One of the women said, "You're wasting your time – if you want to see great plants, come to my garden, it's full of beautiful rose beds." I said, "But I like wild things." And the second woman said, "Well, if you like wild things, then you'll like me." It's a conversation that's stayed with me ever since and my thoughts return to these two women now the book is complete and I wonder what they would make of it. I'd present it to the first woman and hope to convince her of the sheer beauty of working with designed plant communities, using plants that have a natural feel to them. I'd even hope to persuade her that it can be the most beautiful, satisfying and emotionally fulfilling way of working with plants, and for creating complete gardens and landscapes.

But this book is really an imaginary response to the second woman in which I'd tell her that the future is all about planting that's exciting, uplifting, dramatic, beautiful, breath-taking, bold and adventurous. Wild too, and not just in the sense of it being natural but wild because it has an edge to it, it's challenging, it's not safe, and it's not always tasteful.

I don't know where that would go with her but in the spirit of that Australian encounter long ago, I sincerely hope this book starts you on a journey that is truly and exuberantly wild.

Opposite: The Europe Garden in the Queen Elizabeth London Olympic Park, with the grass *Stipa calamagrostis* and red *Lychnis chalcedonica*. Design: Nigel Dunnett and Sarah Price

FURTHER READING

This book is intended to inspire, to whet the appetite, to provide a philosophy, to give an insight into my own projects and planting design ideas. Above all, I wrote it to encourage a spirit of experimentation and to open up a whole realm of possibilities. The books that follow are all excellent companions that will enlarge upon the topics and material I have covered.

Planting: A New Perspective by Piet Oudolf and Noel Kingsbury. Published by Timber Press in 2013. A comprehensive overview of Piet Oudolf's planting design ideas and methods with plant lists to cover most garden situations.

Planting in a Post-Wild World by Thomas Rainer and Claudia West. Published by Timber Press in 2015. A manifesto for a new way of looking at the designed landscape, with in-depth technical information for establishing and managing garden and landscape habitats.

The Dynamic Landscape: Design, Ecology and Management of Urban Naturalistic Vegetation edited by Nigel Dunnett and James Hitchmough. Published by Taylor and Francis in 2007. A wide-ranging and detailed text book on 'designed plant communities' and how to work with them.

Cultivating Chaos by Jonas Reif, Christian Kress and Jurgen Becker. Published by Timber Press in 2015. An ideal opening into the world of ever-changing dynamic gardens and how to manage them.

Planting Design for Dry Gardens by Olivier Filippi. Published by Filbert Press in 2016. A masterful overview of how to adapt dryland plant communities for gardens and designed landscapes. This is just one aspect of the vast unexploited range of natural reference points that are just waiting to be explored.

Planting Green Roofs and Living Walls by Nigel Dunnett and Noel Kingsbury. Published by Timber Press in 2008. In-depth discussion of planting on buildings, and for that matter, low-irrigation, low-fertility diverse plantings in general.

Sowing Beauty by James Hitchmough. Published by Timber Press in 2017. A monograph on creating perennial meadows by seeding and an extensive overview of world grassland vegetation types.

Plant Strategies, Vegetation Processes and Ecosystem Properties by J. Philip Grime. Published by John Wiley & Sons in 2002 (2nd Edition). The best introductory text on ecological theory that is hugely relevant to planting design.

ACKNOWLEDGEMENTS

It's been true since I first started out in my career as a researcher and a designer that most, if not all, of what I do is a result of collaborations with other designers and researchers, and with managers, technicians and gardeners on the ground. I've learnt as much from them as I have from my own experimental work, and I'm hugely grateful to everyone who has worked with me – far too many to list all by name.

I have mentioned people of key influence earlier in the book, but I must single out the American landscape architect Darrel Morrison, whose gentle philosophy of working in tune with nature is one that I have taken to heart and which continually guides my thinking. I have benefitted greatly from the support and encouragement of Piet Oudolf and I am immensely grateful to him for writing the foreword to this book.

My twenty years in the Department of Landscape Architecture at the University of Sheffield, UK, have been marked by the biggest collaboration of them all, with James Hitchmough. We've shared so many ideas and worked to a common set of rules or principles – each of our individual work programmes have informed the other's, culminating in the planting scheme for the London 2012 Olympic Park – an experience that I will never forget. Many PhD students have contributed to the development of my own research, but I must mention two here: Ayako Nagase who supported much of my green roof plant trial work, and who helped to lay the foundations for the roof garden projects in this book, and Jia Yuan who arranged the life-changing trips I have taken to China: the results of these trips feature heavily in the book.

I am indebted to Chris Jones of Telford Borough Council and Dan Cornwell and Sue France of Green Estate in Sheffield who took the Pictorial Meadows idea and made it work on a large scale in challenging urban sites – working alongside people like this has been as crucial to me as any amount of experimental work. Similarly, Michael Walker, Head of Garden and Estate at Trentham, Staffordshire, has been the most wonderful collaborator, always pushing things to be the best they can possibly be. And I have immense gratitude to Bradley Viljoen, Horticultural Officer for the City of London Corporation, for his essential support and steering in the early stages of The Barbican project.

Making gardens for the Chelsea Flower Show has been the most exhilarating experience and has enabled me to promote the messages behind my work to very large audiences. It would not have been possible without the skills and know-how of Mark Gregory, Rich Lavelle and Catherine MacDonald and the whole team at Landform UK: their dedication as landscape contractors and designers in their own right has made a lasting impression on me about the value of teamwork and going the extra mile to make something extraordinary – a heartfelt thank you. Very special thanks go to Taina Suonio who has been my 'right-hand' person in setting out plantings, both in my show gardens but also at the Barbican. None of this would have been possible without my design collaboration with The Landscape Agency who have provided full technical support – thank you to Patrick James, Ed Payne, Rosie Turner and Eleanor Houldcroft.

This book would not have been possible without the vision, clarity, belief (and patience) of my long-term editor and publisher, Anna Mumford. I could not imagine working with anyone else, and it has been the most pleasurable experience to work with her again. I am very grateful for early discussions on the form and content of the book with Sarah Price, with whom I worked on the Olympic Park, and who I have admired ever since for her poetic fusion of art and nature – this again has made a big impression on the way I work.

Finally the greatest thanks go to my family. My wife Dr Marta Herrero has been the most loving and supportive person I could hope for through the whole process of writing this book, and for my two boys, Alex and Jack, both of whom have found their way into the world of horticulture and plants, one as a professional gardener, and one as a landscape architect – I hope it will be as rewarding for them as it has been for me.

Picture acknowledgements
Mark Baldwin/shutterstock.com, page 76 top and middle; Andy Clayden, page 96 top; Karla Dakin, page 30 (top); istock/JFspic, page 72 bottom; istock/sololos, page 119; istock/bingdian, page 164; Jane Sebire, page 14 bottom; Rachel Warne, page 239; Scott Weber, page 168 and 169 bottom; Jan Woudstra, page 56.

INDEX

Page numbers in *italic* type refer to pictures or their captions.

A

Acer pseudoplatanus 114
Achillea
    filipendulina 136, *210–11*
    'Gold Plate' 156
    millefolium 159, *214*, *218*
    'Moonshine' 122
    'Paprika' 158
    'Summer Wine' 156
    'Terracotta' *196–7*, 199
acidic soils 103
African love grass see *Eragrostis curvula*
aggregation patterns 80, 93–4, *93–4*, 111, 118, 121, *194*
Alchemilla mollis 122
alder see *Alnus*
Allium 132, 136, 199, *200*, *216*
    'Globemaster' *131*, *139*
    schoenoprasum 185, *186–7*
    ursinum 27
Alnus 80
Alpine plants 103
Amelanchier 199
    lamarckii 190, 193
American garden movement 68
Ammi majus 40–1, *132*, *163*
Amstelveen Heem Parks 48, 49–51, *49–51*, *58*, 67, 81, *108*, 114
anchor plants 111, 123
    character anchors 126, *126–7*
    framework anchors 123, 144, *198*
    matrix anchors 123, *124–7*, *136*, 144, *145*, *194*
    primary and secondary 126
Andropogon geradii 158
Anemone
    appenina 160–1
    x *hybrida* 148, *148*
    nemorosa 27, 50
annuals 101, *102*, 130, *132*, 138, *140*
    seeding 212, 218
Anthemis tinctoria 187, *212*
Anthriscus sylvestris 45
apple see *Malus*
Appleton, Jay
    The Experience of Landscape 20
Aquilegia
    canadensis 120
    vulgaris 45, *132*, *189*
Armeria maritima 179
Artemisia 86
Arts and Crafts movement 60–1, *61*, 66

ash see *Fraxinus*
Aster 185
    amellus 199
    divaricatus 115
    x *frikartii* 'Mönch' *188*
    macrophyllus 115, *116–17*, *158*, *217*
    novibelgii 102
    'Purple Dome' 122
    tongolensis 92–3
Astilbe chinensis var. *taquetii*
    'Purpurlanze' 172, *172*

B

Barbican, London 11, *17*, 21, *31*, 69, 162, *226*
    Beech Gardens *123*, *129*, *136*, 190–2, *190–201*, *198–9*, *213*
    stairwell entrances 152
    steppe plantings 126, *131*, *162*, 198, *198–9*, *227*
bedstraw
    hedge see *Galium mollugo*
    lady's see *Galium verum*
beech see *Fagus*
berberis 78
Bergenia 'Rotblum' 158
Betula 50, 80, *194*
    albo-sinensis 149
    nigra 104, *153*
    pendula 101, *102*
Bibury Road Verges 46–7, *47*
biennials 130, *133*
biodiversity 48, 83, 85, 96, 103, *152*, 186, 202–3, *202–7*, 226
    dominator plants 100–1, *101*, 103
    green infrastructure 174, 192
    log piles *152*, 202–3, *202–5*
biogeographic plantings 15, 63–4, *72*
biophilic design 166
birch see *Betula*
Bishop's flower see *Ammi majus*
bioswales 170–1, *171*, *179*
blue moor grass see *Sesleria nitida*
blue oat grass see *Helicotrichon sempervirens*
Blue Ridge Parkway, North Carolina *46*
blue tansy see *Phaecelia tanacetifolia*
bluebell see *Hyacinthoides non-scripta*
boundaries see edges
box see *Buxus semperivirens*
Briza minor 27
Brown, Capability 55–6, *55*
Brunnera macrophylla 'Jack Frost' *126*, *151*
brush 78–9

Buckingham Palace, Diamond Garden 150, *151*, 152
bulbs 130, *131*
Buphthalmum salicifolium 134–5
Burke, Edmund
    A Philosophical Enquiry 56
BUSarchitecktur & BOA 157
butterbur see *Petasites hybridus*
Buxus sempervirens 109, *110*, 149

C

Calamagrostis
    x *acutiflora* 'Overdam' *189*
    x *acutiflora* 'Karl Foerster' *127*, *136*, 148, *148–9*, *176*, *178*, *179*
    brachytricha 149, *111*
Californian poppy see *Eschscholtzia californica*
Caltha palustris 51, 59, *88*
Cammassia 216
Campanula lactiflora 'Loddon Anna' *111*, 203
campion see *Silene*
Cardamine pratensis 26
Castanea sativa 45, 228
ceiling layer plant communities 80–1, *80–1*, 107, 109
Centaurea 212
    cyanus 'Black Ball' *132*
    nigra 87, *218*
    scabiosa 27, *145*, 159, *212*
central reservations 33
Centranthus ruber 73, *186*
centre of gravity (COG) aggregation pattern 80, 93–4, *93–4*, 111, 118, 121, *194*
    anchor plants 111, 123, *123*
    satellite plants 123, 128, *128–9*, *194*
Cephalaria gigantea 144–5
Chamerion angustifolium 101
chaos 20
chaparral 78
character anchor plants 126, *126–7*
Chatsworth House *55*
Chelsea Flower Show
    biodiverse gardens 204–5, *205*
    North American woodland planting *120*
cherry see *Prunus*
China
    garden tradition 54
    meadow plants 15, 44, *44*, 82–5, *82–6*, *88*, 90–5
chives see *Allium schoenoprasum*
Chongqing *167*
Church, Thomas

Gardens are for People 58
Clematis 79
climate change 165, 169, 170–1, 191
clonal plants 137
clump-forming plants 137, *214*, 218
colour 61–2, *152*, *154–61*, 155
    colour-themed seed mixes *212*
    impressionistic naturalism 68
    repetition 156
    visual coherence 30–1, *31*
community involvement 199
competitive compatibility 137
competitor (dominator) plants 100–1, *101*, 103, 137, 210
Convallaria major 50
coppicing 45, *45*, 48, *108*, 109, *110*, 228–9
    coppice management 228
Coreopsis 212
cornflower see *Centaurea*
Cornus 228
Corydalis solida 50
Corylus avellana 45, *146*, 228, *229*
cosmos 42–3
Cotinus coggygria 95
cow parsley see *Anthriscus sylvestris*
cowslip see *Primula veris*
Crataegus monogyna 78, *79*, 79, 144
Crocosmia
    x *crocosmiiflora* 'George Davison' 172, *172*
    'Emberglow' *158*
    'Lucifer' *196–7*
cross-over species 92, *92*, 114, 121, *194*
cultivation 101
cultural context 98–9, *99*
Cynoglossum amabile 84, *93*

D

Daucus carota 136, *141*, *220–1*
derelict plots *32*, 33, *102*, *133*
    dominator plants 100–1, *101*, 103
Deschampsia cespitosa 115, *124–5*, *126*, *129*, 144, 159, *179*, 203
desert blooms 101
designing plant distribution 118–63
    anchor plants 111, 123, *123–7*, *126*, *194*
    compatibility 137, *152*
    free-floating plants 123, 130, *130–5*
    layering 142, *142–5*
    plant forms 137
    pop-up plants 101, *102*, 137, *162*, 212
    satellite plants 123, 128, *128–9*, *194*
Dianthus carthusianorum 134–5, *141*, 189

Dictamnus albus 98
Digitalis purpurea 203, *203*
Dipsacus fullonum 110
direction *see* flow
disturbance, plant strategy theory 100–3, 121
dogwood *see Cornus*
dominator plants 100–1, *101*, 103, 137, 210
Dove Cottage Nursery, Yorkshire 154
drifts 90–1, *90–2*, 93, 114, 116, 121
    repetition 95, *95*
dry plantings 182, *182–201*, 211
Dryopteris wallichiana 116
Duisburg 72
Dunnett, Nigel
    Rain Gardens 170
durable (stress-tolerator) plants 103, 137
Dutch modernism 58, *58*, 66, 67
dynamic management 162–3, 198

E

Echinacea
    pallida 154, 158
    paradoxa 158
    purpurea 154, 158, 217
Echinops ritro 'Veitch's Blue' 199
Echium vulgare 158
ecological conditions 45
ecological fitness 31
ecological horticulture 63
ecology 121
ecotones 96, *96–7*
Edelman, Edith 46
edges 91, 96, *96–7*, 114, 121
elder *see Sambucus*
emergents 95, *95*, 120, *120*, *136*, 152
emotional response, creating 10, *14*, 16, 20, 28–9
Epimedium 116
Eragrostis curvula 123
Eremurus stenophyllus 138, 141
Erodium manescavii 131, 185
Eryngium 154
    yuccifolium 104
Eschscholtzia californica 102, 130
Eupatorium
    cannabinum 'Flore Pleno' 179
    hyssopifolium 104
    'Purple Bush' 156
Euphorbia
    characias ssp *wulfenii* 123, 129, 158, 191, 194, 227
    cyparissias 96, 185
    jolkinii 82–4, 86, 93

    palustris 51, *127*, 142–3, 144, *144–5*
    polychroma 194
    wulfenii 136, 199, 203
evening primrose *see Oenothera biennis*

F

Fagus sylvatica 80, 147
feather grass *see Stipa pennata*
fertilizers 48
Festuca
    amethystina 185
    ovina 214
Filipendula ulmaria 156, 177
fitness to site 152
flax *see Linum perenne*
floor layer plant communities 76–7, *76–7*, 107, 109
flow 90–1, *90*, 106, *106*, 120
    flowing spaces 108
    lines 111–14, 116, 152
    Universal FLOW model 69, 120–1
'flowery mead' 54
Foeniculum vulgare 139
Foerster, Karl 63, 67
forces, Universal FLOW model 120–1, 137
formal elements 25, 29, 30, 108, 147, 152, 174
formal gardens 52, 54, 55
Forsythia 110
fox and cubs *see Hieracium aurantiacum*
foxglove *see Digitalis purpurea*
foxtail lily *see Eremurus stenophyllus*
framework anchor plants 123, *123*, 144, 198
framing 146
Fraxinus 80
free-floating plants 123, 130, *130–5*, 194
fumewort *see Corydalis solida*
fungi 203
fynbos 78

G

Galium
    mollugo 159, 218, 228
    verum 76, 220–1
Garden House, Devon 123
Gaura lindheimeri 179
Geranium
    x *cantabrigiense* 'St Ola' 151
    macrorrhizum 110, 151
    maculatum 'Elizabeth Anne' 120
    psilostemon 228
    'Rozanne' 224
    sylvaticum 110, 224

Germany
    new perennial movement 47
    technocratic naturalism 63, 67
giant fleabane *see Inula magnifica*
Gilpin, William 56
golden rod *see Solidago*
gradients, environmental 92, *92*
grassland plant communities 17, *19*, 76, *76–7*, 109
    see also meadow plant communities
    boundaries 91
    flows and drifts 90–1, *90–2*, 93
    layering 88, *88–9*
    phenology 86–7, *86*, 88
    savannah vegetation 17, *19*, 80
    succession 88
    wood pasture 98
Gravetye Manor 54
grazing line 98
great burnet *see Sanguisorba officinalis*
Great Dixter 25, 61, 132
green infrastructure 166–7, 174, *174–5*
green roofs 182, *182*
Greening Grey Britain campaign 167
Greig-Smith, Peter
    Quantitative Plant Ecology 94
Grime, Philip 46, 100
growth forms 137

H

Hackfall, North Yorkshire 56, *57*
Hansen, Richard and Stahl, Freidrich
    Perennials and their Garden Habitats 63
Hauser and Wirth, Somerset 68
hawthorn *see Crataegus monogyna*
hay meadows 48
hazel *see Corylus avellana*
heathland 76, 78–9, *78–9*, 103
hedges 144, *145*, 147, 149, 174
Helianthus decapetalus 76
Helicotrichon sempervirens 126, 185, 189, 199
Hemerocallis 'Whichford' 172
herbaceous layer 76
heron's bill *see Erodium manescavii*
Hesperis matronalis 45, 132
Hieracium aurantiacum 186
hierarchy of needs 29–31, 54, 56
High Line, New York 10, *11*
high-impact, low-input planting 16, 48
highway edges 33
Hilton, James
    The Lost Horizon 82

Hitchmough, James 47–8, *47*, 64, 106, 158
    London Olympic Park 35, *134–5*, 147, 214
    prairie meadow 48, 64
    Sowing Beauty 15, 64, *212*
Hogarth, William
    line of beauty 111
honesty *see Lunaria biennis*
Hopkins, John 35
Hordeum jubatum 158
hortus conclusus 54
Hosta 'Tall Boy' 149
human evolutionary history 19–20, *19*, 28
human scale 10, 18–20, *18*, *21*
Hyacinthoides non-scripta 26, 27, 229
hyssopleaf thoroughwort *see Eupatorium hyssopifolium*

I

immersive experiences 97, *97*, 109, *152*, 201
impressionistic naturalism 59, 60–1, *60–1*, 68–9
insertion mix 114
intimate spaces 10, 18–20, *18*, *19*, *21*, 29
    hortus conclusus 54
Inula magnifica 177
Iris 148
    bulleyana 15, 84–5, 93
    'Mrs Rowe' 172
    sibirica 172, 179, 224

J

James, Rosanna 60–1
Jekyll, Gertrude 46, 60–1, 67
    Wood and Garden 59
Jensen, Jens 68
    Siftings 28
John Lewis Rain Garden, London 174, *174–5*, 211
Juncus effusus 179

K

Kings Cross, London 112–13
Klee, Paul 155
knapweed
    black *see Centaurea nigra*
    greater *see Centaurea scabiosa*
Knautia
    arvensis 27, *27*
    macedonica 131, 156, 159, 199
Knight, Richard Payne 56

Kniphofia 122, *139*, *141*, 184
    'Green Jade' *188*
    'Tawny King' *158*, *199*
    triangularis *138*, *179*
Korn, Peter *211*

L

lady's smock see *Cardamine pratensis*
Lamprocapnos (*Dicentra*) *spectabilis* 116
layering 81, 88, *106–8*, *116*, 123, 142, *142–5*
    Universal FLOW model 120–1
LDA Design and Hargreaves Associates 35
legibility 30–1, *31*, 68, 78, 111, 152
Leucanthemum
    x *superbum* *128*, *145*, *156*, *159*
    vulgare 73, 87, *159*, *218*, *224*
Libertia *136*
    formosa *122*, *193*
lichens 94
Ligularia
    macrophylla *86*
    'The Rocket' *172*
Ligustrum 78, *79*
lily of the valley see *Convallaria major*
lime see *Tilia*
Linaria purpurea 102, *186*, *187*, 212
line 111–14, 116, 152
    framework anchor plants 123
Linum perenne *158*, *219*
Liquidambar styraciflua *75*
Liriodendron tulipifera *153*
Lloyd, Christopher
    The Well-Tempered Garden 24
London Wetland Centre Rain Garden 176, *176–7*
Lunaria biennis 45
Lurie Garden, Chicago 67
Luzula sylvatica *151*
Lychnis
    chalcedonica *129*, *145*, *230*
    coronaria 'Alba' *131*, *159*, *196–7*
    flos-cuculi 'White Robin' *172*
Lythrum salicaria *127*, *145*, *172*, *173*, 176

M

maintenance
    dynamic management 162–3, 198
    meadows 223, *225*
    perennials 226–7, *226–7*
    weed control 210, 212, 216, 218, 222, 223
Malus 79, *99*, *158*

Malva moschata 'Alba' *156*, *159*
maquis 78
marsh marigold see *Caltha palustris*
marsh spurge see *Euphorbia palustris*
Maslow, Abraham
    'Hierarchy of Needs' 29–31
mass-space plan 106–7, *106–8*
matrix anchor plants 123, *124–7*, *136*, 144, *145*, 194
Matteuccia struthiopteris 229
meadows 15, 76, 137, *216*
    boundaries 91, *96–7*
    Chinese reference meadow 82–5, *82–6*, *88*, *90–5*
    flows and drifts 90–1, *90–2*, 93
    grasses 218
    layering 88, *89–9*
    maintenance 223, *225*
    phenology 86–7, *86*, 88
    plant density 212, 218
    plant growth forms 137
    planting perennials 222, *224*
    pre-grown meadow turf 222, *223*
    seeding 212, *212*, *214–21*, 218
    soil fertility 210, *225*
    succession 88
meadowsweet see *Filipendula ulmaria*
meandering lines 90, *90*, 111, 114
medieval gardens 54
Melbourne *182*
Melica ciliata *131*, *158*
Miscanthus
    'Kleine Silberspinne' *136*
    sinensis 'Undine' *136*, *148*, *193*, *199*
modernism 58, *58*, 59
modernistic naturalism 59, 63, 64, 66–9, *66–8*
Molinia caerulea 67
monarch of the veldt see *Venidium fastuosum*
monotony 16, 17, 91, 137
Moorgate Crofts roof terrace, Rotherham 63, 184, *184–5*
Morrison, Darrel 68, 106–7
movement see flow
mulches 210, *211*, 216
Munstead Wood 59

N

Nassauer, Joan
    'Messy Ecosystems, Orderly Frames' 29
native plant movements 15
natural plant communities 72–81, *72–81*
naturalism 10, 15, 17, 54, 56, 106

Arts and Crafts movement 60–1, *61*, 66
    contemporary 59–69
    enhanced nature 60
    immersive experience 31, 97, *97*, 109
    impressionistic 59, 60–1, *60–1*, 68–9
    making spaces 106–7
    modernistic 59, 63, 64, 66–9, *66–8*
    random planting 63, 64, *64*, 69, 118, 120, 121, 209
    technocratic 59, 63–4, *63–5*, 67, 68–9, 93, 118, 121
naturalistic planting 10–11, 59
naturalization 60, *224*
naturalized plants 72, *73*, 73
Nepeta 157
    'Dawn to Dusk' *156*, *159*
Netherlands
    Amstelveen Heem Parks 48, 49–51, *49–51*, 58, 67, 81, *108*, 114
    Dutch modernism 58, *58*, 66, 67
New American Garden movement 46
new perennial planting 10–11, 47, 59
non-native plants 45, 47
North American Michaelmas daisy see *Aster novibelgii*

O

oak see *Quercus*
Oehme, Wolfgang 68
Oenothera biennis 25
Olympic Park, London *8*, 33, 35, *158*, *212*, 214
    Asia Garden 148, *148–9*
    California Bank *130*
    Europe Garden *128*, *142–5*, 144, *227*, *230*
    Fantasticology Area 64, *214*, 218, *218–21*, *225*
    North American Garden *136*, *227*
    Olympic Gold Meadows 35–7, *215*
    Southern Hemisphere Garden *147*
    Stitch Meadows *134–5*, *136*, 138, *138–41*
orchards 99, 109
order 120–1, 146–53, *146–53*, 174
    colour 152, *154–61*, 155
    external 146, *146–51*, 152
    internal 146, 152
    transparency 159, *159*
Oreganum laevigatum 'Herrenhausen' *199*
organic weed control 210
organizational structure 118–63
    Universal FLOW model 120–1

Osmunda regalis 51, *51*
Oudolf, Piet 66–7, *66–8*
oxeye daisy see *Leucanthemum vulgare*
oxlip see *Primula elatoir*

P

painterly planting design 61, *212*
pampas grassland 76
Papaver orientale *139*, *201*
pasque flower see *Pulsatilla vulgaris*
Pearson, Dan 62, *136*
Pedicularis siphonantha *84*, *93*
perennial forget-me-not see *Brunnera*
perennials
    coppicing and 228, *228–9*
    maintenance regime 226–7, *226–7*
    meadow plantings 222, *224*
    naturalistic plantings 63
    seed mixes 137, 212, *212*, *214*, 216, 218, *218–21*, 223
    short-lived 130, *131*, 133
Perovskia
    atriplicifolia *139*, *199*
    'Blue Spire' *188*
Persicaria
    amplexicaulis 148, *224*, 228
    bistorta 15, *84*, *110*, *224*
Petasites hybridus 26
Phacelia tanacetifolia *102*
phenology 86–7, *86*, 88, 142
Phlomis *136*, *199*
    fruticosa *158*
    russeliana *193*
Phlox 89, 114
    divaricata 76, *120*
Phragmites communis 'Variegata' *176*
Pictorial Meadows *8*, *14*, 33–5, *33*, *34–43*, 50, *187*, 223
pictorial planting 50–1, *50–1*
Picturesque movement 55–6, *56*, *57*, 58, 59, 60, 146
pillars and columns 79, *96*, 109, 123, *146*
Pitmedden 55
plant association 61–2, *61*, 69
plant communities 15, *16–17*, *16*, 48, 64, 68, 72–3, 106
    boundaries 91
    ceiling layer 80–1, *80–1*, 107, 109
    cross-over species 92, *92*, 114, 121, 194
    designed 162
    environmental gradients 92, *92*
    floor layer 76–7, *76–7*, 107, 109
    flows and drifts 90–1, *90–2*, 93
    meadows 15, 76, 82–5, *82–6*, 88, *90–1*

natural 72-81, *72-81*
naturalized plants 72, 73, *73*
plant compatibility 137, 152
productivity and stability 100-3
recombinant 73, *73*
reference communities 76-81
shrubs 78-9, *78-9*, 109
walls layer 75, 78-9, *78-9*, 107, 109
woodland 80-1, *80-1*
plant diversity 83, 85, 96, 103, 121
plant ecology 121
plant growth forms 121
plant mixes, designing 121
plant signatures 99
plant sociability 93
Plant Strategy Theory 46, 100-3, 121
plant structural types 121, 123
planting density 212, *213*, 217, 218
plug plants 222
pollution 165
polyanthus *see Primula polyantha*
pop-up plants 101, *102*, 137, *162*, 212
Portland 168-9
Potentilla chinensis 95
prairie dropseed *see Sporobulus heterolepis*
prairie grassland 76, 89, 97
Price, Sarah 62, *128*, 142-5, *144*, *147*, *158*, *230*
Price, Uvedale 56
primrose *see Primula vulgaris*
Primula
  elatior 50, *229*
  florindae 176
  poissonii 82-3, 88, *93*
  polyantha 45
  sikkimensis 84
  veris 47, 184, *185*, 198
  vulgaris 27, 45, 50, *116*
privet *see Ligustrum*
productivity and stability 100-3
prospect (sight-lines) 19, 20, *20*, 78
Prunus 80, *136*
  serrula 133
  'Sunset Boulevard' *190*, 193
Pulmonaria 116
  'Cotton Cool' *126*
Pulsatilla vulgaris 184, *185*, 198
purple loosestrife *see Lythrum salicaria*
purple toadflax *see Linaria purpurea*

Q

quaking grass, lesser *see Briza minor*
Quercus 80, *81*, 107, 114

R

rain gardens 169, 170-8, *171-81*, *207*, 211
Rainer, Thomas and West, Claudia
  Planting in a Post-Wild World 63
random planting method 63, 64, *64*, 69, 118, 120, 121, 209
  structural plants 69, 120
rattlesnake master *see Eryngium yuccifolium*
Raulston, JC 46
recombinant plant communities 73, *73*
reference plant communities 76-81, 109
refuge (cover) 19, 20, *20*, 78
repetition 30, 95, *95*, 146, 152, 156
Repton, Humphrey 56
Resedea luteola 102, *133*
Rheum palmatum atrosanguineum 133
Rhododendron 78, 114
rhubarb *see Rheum palmatum atrosanguineum*
Rhus typhina 228, *228*
rhythm and repetition 30, 95, *95*, 152
right plant, right place 60
road-side plantings 216
Robinson, William 67
  The Wild Garden 60
Rodgersia pinnata 'Superba' 177
roof gardens 182, *182-7*, 184, 186, 190-2, *190-201*, 198-9
Rosa 78, 79
  spinosissima 61
rosebay willowherb *see Chamerion angustifolium*
rowan *see Sorbus*
royal fern *see Osmunda regalis*
Rubus 79
  odoratus 110
Rudbeckia
  fulgida var. *deamii* 158, 172, *172*, 179, 203, *217*, 228
  laciniata 46
ruderals (pop-ups) 101
ruins, Picturesque 56, *56*, *57*
Russian sage *see Perovskia atriplicifolia*
Ruys, Mien 66-7

S

Salix 78, *108*, 228
Salvia 136
  nemorosa 76, *129*, 156-7, *158*, 196-7, 199, *201*
Sambucus 79
Sanguisorba officinalis 87, *145*
Sarcococca confusa 174

satellite plants 123, 128, *128-9*, 194
savannah vegetation 17, *19*, 80, 109
scabious
  devil's bit *see Succisa pratensis*
  field *see Knautia arvensis*
  giant *see Centaurea scabiosa*
Schmidt, Cassian 64
Scilla messeniaca 160-1
Scott Arboretum, Philadelphia 153
scrubland 76, 78-9, *78-9*, 86, 109
sea thrift *see Armeria maritima*
seasonal changes 86-7
sedges 106
seeding, cultivation by 137, 212, *212*, *214-21*, 218
  combining with planting 217
  ensuring even distribution 218
  seed mixes 121
  sowing rate 218
semi-natural landscapes 74, *74*, 98-9, 99
Senecio 88
Sesleria nitida 126, *136*, *194*, 199
setting-out density 212, *213*
sheep's fescue *see Festuca ovina*
Sheffield 30, 35, 44, 73
  Botanical Gardens 229
  General Cemetery 109
  Grey to Green Project 178, *178-81*, 211
  rain gardens 169
  ring road planting 216
  Sharrow School roof garden 186, *186-7*
Sheffield University 46-8, 64, 100
  Garden of Pooled Talents 188, *188-9*
shrubs 78-9, *78-9*, 91, 109
  emergents 95, *95*
  as framework anchors 123
shuttlecock fern *see Matteuccia struthiopteris*
Silene
  armeria 187
  dioica 219
  fimbriata 116, *133*
  uniflora 185
  vulgaris 45
Silphium perfoliatum 89
Singapore 166, *182*
Sissinghurst Castle, Kent *136*, 160-1, 229
Sisyrinchium striatum 158, *185*, *201*
site analysis 106, 121
site preparation 210, *210*
Sleightholmedale Lodge, Yorkshire 60-1
small spaces 10, 18-20, *18*, *21*, 96
smoke bush *see Cotinus coggygria*
soil fertility 103, 137, 210, *225*

Solidago 158, *228*
Sorbus 80
space, structuring and shaping 17, 106-15, *106-8*
  flowing sequence 111
  structural plants 120
speedwell *see Veronica officinalis*
Sporobolus heterolepis 104, 107, *136*
spreading plants 137
squirrel grass *see Hordeum jubatum*
stable environments 100-3
Stachys
  betonica 87, *211*
  byzantina 185
Stellera chamaejasme var. *chrysantha* 94
steppe grassland 76, *76*, 98, *126*, 131, *158*, 182, *185*, 198
Stipa
  calamagrostis 124-5, *128-9*, *136*, *145*, *159*, *231*
  pennata 76
stress, plant strategy theory 100-3, 121, 137
structure
  ceiling layer 80-1, *80-1*, 107, 109
  flows and drifts 90-1, *90-2*, 93
  layering 81, 88
  organizational 118-63
  structural plants 69, 75-81, 98, 111, 123, 144
  walls layer 75, 78-9, *78-9*, 107, 109
Stuart-Smith, Tom 61, 62, *62*, 146, *147*
sublime, response to 30, 31, 56
succession 88
Succisa pratensis 127, *145*, 172, *173*
sumach *see Rhus typhina*
sustainable drainage systems (SuDS) 169, 170-8, *171-81*, *207*, 211
swales 170-1, *171*, 179
sweet chestnut *see Castanea sativa*
sweet rocket *see Hesperis matronalis*
sycamore *see Acer pseudoplatanus*

T

taxonomic approach 15
teasel *see Dipsacus fullonum*
technocratic naturalism 59, 63-4, *63-5*, 67, 68-9, 93, 118, 121
Thalictrum 148
  delavayi 149
  'Elin' 203
thinleaf sunflower *see Helianthus decapetalus*
Tiarella 114, 116
  cordifolia 'Spring Symphony' 116

Tilia 80
Townsend Landscape Architects *147*
traditional horticulture 24, *24*, 47
transparency 159, *159*
trees
    see also woodland
    ceiling layer 80-1, *80-1*, 109
    COG aggregation pattern 80, 94, 118, 121
    coppicing 45, *45*, 48, *108*, 109, *110*, 228
    as framework anchors 123
    structural plants 98
    urban environments 166-7
    woodland edges 96, *96*
Trentham Gardens, Staffordshire 155
    Italian Garden *52*, *62*, *146*
    perennial meadow 65, *124-5*, *129*, *156*, *159*, *223*
    planted meadow *213*
    river of grass *66-7*
    seeded meadow *38-41*, *102*
    woodland garden 114, *115-17*, *126*, *133*, *158*
Trillium 114, *229*
tulip tree see *Liriodendron tulipifera*
Tulipa
    praestans *190*, *194*, *198*
    turkestanica *198*
tundra 76
tuned to nature 10

U

Universal FLOW model 69, 120-1
universal planting 118
urban environments 14, *21*, *122*, *133*, 166-7
    community involvement 199
    dry plantings 182, *182-201*
    green infrastructure 166-7, *169*, 174, *174-5*, 178, *178-81*
    modernism 58
    modernistic naturalism 67, 68
    natural plant communities 72-3, *72-3*
    naturalistic plantings 47
    Pictorial Meadows 33-4, *33*
    podium landscapes 188, 190
    roof gardens 182, *182-7*, 184, 186, 190-2, *190-201*, 198-9
urbanization 165, 166-7
user analysis 106

V

van Sweden, James 68
Venidium fastuosum *132*
Verbascum *136*, *141*, 186
    'Sixteen Candles' *139*
Verbena bonariensis *127*, *138-9*, *141*, *156*, *159*
Veronica officinalis 87
Viburnum 79
Vienna University Business School *157*
viewing points 111
Viola odorata 27, 45, *50*
violet see *Viola odorata*
viper's bugloss see *Echium vulgare*
Viscaria 140
    oculta *163*
visual coherence 30-1, *31*
visual ecology 72-3

W

wall valerian see *Centranthus ruber*
walls layer plant communities 75, 78-9, *78-9*, 107
water-sensitive design 169, 170-8, *171-81*, *207*, *211*
watering 212
waves 120-1, *142*, *162-3*
Weber, Scott *168-9*
weeds 101
    controlling 210, 212, *216*, *218*, 222, *223*
weld see *Resedea luteola*
wetlands 76, *77*, 109, 176, *176-7*
whitebeam see *Sorbus*
wild carrot see *Daucus carota*
wild garlic see *Allium ursinum*
wildlife see biodiversity
Wiley, Keith 123
willow see *Salix*
Wisley, Surrey 61, *147*
    prairie meadow *48*, *64*
witch hazel *160-1*
wood anemones see *Anemone nemorosa*
wood pasture *98*, 109
wood rush see *Luzula sylvatica*
woodland 80-1, *80-1*, 109
    see also coppicing; trees
    dark 80-1, *81*, 109
    edges 96, *96*, 109, *110*, 198
    layering *81*, 88, *107*, *108*
    light 80-1, *80*, 109
    North American *116*, *120*
    pioneer 80, 109
    Trentham woodland garden 114, *115-17*
    wildflowers 26, 27
woody plants 78-9

Y

yarrow see *Achillea*
yucca *211*

ABOUT THE AUTHOR

Nigel Dunnett is one of the world's leading voices on planting design. As plantsman, designer and pioneer of the naturalistic or ecological approach to planting, he creates gardens and public landscapes that teem with plants and wildlife, bring multiple environmental benefits and enrich people's lives. Science and art come together in his approach that draws on decades of experimental work and close collaboration with architects and artists to create gardens that are dramatic and beautiful as well as being fully functioning, sustainable plant communities.

Notable examples include his extensive new woodland and meadow plantings at Trentham Gardens in Staffordshire; the Beech Gardens and High Walk at the Barbican Centre in London which are brilliant exemplars of 'designed plant communities' (and won both the Landscape Institute's Planting Design Award 2018 and the Landscape Institute Fellows' Award 2018 for most outstanding project); and the London 2012 Olympic Park (now the Queen Elizabeth Olympic Park) where huge swathes of brightly coloured meadows first changed our perceptions about public planting.

Nigel is dedicated to bringing his ideas and methodology to a wide audience as evidenced by this book and by his responsibilities as ambassador of the RHS campaign 'Greening Grey Britain' and Professor of Planting Design and Vegetative Ecology at Sheffield University. His award-winning show gardens for RHS flower shows at Chelsea (Gold Medal 2013) and Hampton Court showcase green roofs, rainwater harvesting and ecological planting and have inspired many gardeners. He is author of several books on his specialist subjects and lectures at universities, design schools and plant societies throughout the world.